Improving Thinking in the Classroom

Programs like philosophy for children, reciprocal teaching, problem based learning and computerized games can help students' critical and creative thinking skills, but which are most effective? This research-to-practice book showcases how you can improve the thinking (cognition) of your students, across the curriculum and beyond.

Each chapter focuses on a particular program, describes the method and background research, offers examples and explains key processes in implementation. You'll learn about thinking programs within a subject, across the curriculum, outside the curriculum and those which can be either within or outside the curriculum, so you can choose a program which suits your context.

You'll also find out what to consider when evaluating a thinking skills program. And finally, you'll discover shared features of the methods – such as peer interaction, discourse, argumentation, scaffolding and transfer – so you can see the commonalities of the programs and think about designing your own approaches.

Whether you're a classroom teacher, department head, or other key stakeholder, this powerful resource will help you determine what really works for teaching thinking, so your students can apply such skills and thrive long after they've left school.

Note: This book is part of a set; a companion book focuses on programs for teaching metacognition, or thinking about thinking.

Keith J. Topping is an educator, researcher, author and international speaker. His interests are peer learning, parents as educators, social competence, computer-assisted assessment and inclusion. Topping has written 27 books and more than 400 other publications, including 200 peer-reviewed journal papers.

Also Available from Routledge Eye on Education

(routledge.com/k-12)

Improving Thinking About Thinking in the Classroom: What Works for Enhancing Metacognition
Keith J. Topping

Improving Reading Comprehension of Self-Chosen Books through Computer Assessment and Feedback: Best Practices from Research
Keith J. Topping

The Student Motivation Handbook: 50 Ways to Boost an Intrinsic Desire to Learn
Larry Ferlazzo

Passionate Learners, 3rd Edition: How to Engage and Empower Your Students
Pernille Ripp

Rigor Is Not a Four-Letter Word, 3rd Edition
Barbara R. Blackburn

Improving Thinking in the Classroom
What Works for Enhancing Cognition

Keith J. Topping

Routledge
Taylor & Francis Group

NEW YORK AND LONDON

Designed cover image: © Getty Images

First published 2024
by Routledge
605 Third Avenue, New York, NY 10158

and by Routledge
4 Park Square, Milton Park, Abingdon, Oxon, OX14 4RN

Routledge is an imprint of the Taylor & Francis Group, an informa business

© 2024 Keith J. Topping

The right of Keith J. Topping to be identified as author of this work has been asserted in accordance with sections 77 and 78 of the Copyright, Designs and Patents Act 1988.

All rights reserved. No part of this book may be reprinted or reproduced or utilised in any form or by any electronic, mechanical, or other means, now known or hereafter invented, including photocopying and recording, or in any information storage or retrieval system, without permission in writing from the publishers.

Trademark notice: Product or corporate names may be trademarks or registered trademarks, and are used only for identification and explanation without intent to infringe.

ISBN: 978-1-032-51432-1 (hbk)
ISBN: 978-1-032-51289-1 (pbk)
ISBN: 978-1-003-40218-3 (ebk)

DOI: 10.4324/9781003402183

Typeset in Palatino
by SPi Technologies India Pvt Ltd (Straive)

Contents

1 Introduction 1

SECTION A   Programs Within a Traditional Subject 15

2 Science: Cognitive Acceleration Through Science
   Education (CASE) 17

3 Mathematics: Cognitively Guided Instruction in
   Mathematics (CGI) 28

4 Reading: Paired Reading and Thinking 49

5 Geography: Thinking Through Geography (TTG) 61

**SECTION B   Programs Across the Traditional
              Curriculum** 75

6 Reciprocal Teaching (RT) 77

7 Activating Children's Thinking Skills (ACTS) 90

8 Thinking Actively in Social Contexts (TASC) 102

**SECTION C   Programs Outside the Traditional
              Curriculum** 121

9 Instrumental Enrichment (IE) 123

10 CoRT (Cognitive Research Trust) 137

SECTION D Programs Either Within or Outside the Traditional Curriculum **161**

11 Philosophy for Children (P4C)........................163

12 Problem-Based Learning (PBL) 181

13 Educational Games..................................196

SECTION E Evaluation, Discussion and Conclusion **207**

14 Evaluating Thinking Skills Development..............209

15 Discussion and Conclusions..........................220

Appendix 1 224
Appendix 2 238

1

Introduction

The aim of this book is to help teachers improve the thinking skills of their students/pupils, not just in a narrowly focused area but across the curriculum and beyond it, with a view to preparing them for the world beyond education. Long after they have forgotten the detailed knowledge they were taught, the students' refined and widely applicable ability to think should help them perform better in a job or profession and help them solve everyday problems in their personal life, leading to becoming a happier person with a greater sense of well-being.

This book is one of a pair published at the same time with closely related themes. Both books draw on research evidence for the effectiveness of the various methods suggested. Then implementation guidelines are given to teachers, before the common threads of the methods are drawn together in a discussion and conclusion. The first book (this book) is called *Improving Thinking in the Classroom: What Works for Enhancing Cognition*. The second book is called *Improving Thinking About Thinking in the Classroom: What Works for Enhancing Metacognition*. The first is about matters that teachers consider frequently. The second is about matters that teachers consider less frequently. The hope is that teachers might read the first book and be inspired to read the second book.

What Is Thinking?

Given that the aim of this book is to improve thinking skills, that means improving quantity (the amount of time spent thinking) and quality (the depth or intensity or complexity of thinking). Of course, we might start by asking, "What do we mean by thinking?"

The *Oxford English Dictionary* describes thinking as active conception in the mind; considering and forming connected ideas or reasoning about something; apprehending clearly; reflecting and judging; trying to solve problems. Thinking is the ability to focus attention, process information, store and retrieve memories and select appropriate responses and actions. Thinking is also the capacity for abstraction, logic, understanding, reasoning, planning, creativity and critical thinking. Well, that seems like a good start.

However, as Presseisen (1986) noted, the history of the attempt to define thinking is "without a complete and exact end". Focusing on "critical thinking", she discusses Glaser's work on inferences, assumptions, deductive reasoning, drawing conclusions and evaluating arguments.

The Cornell Critical Thinking Tests in 1985 examined seven areas: induction, deduction, value judgment, observation, credibility, assumptions and meaning. Eisner proposed variables of questioning, speculating, evaluating and constructing. Dismissing the vague term "higher-order thinking", Resnick felt that high-quality thinking was non-algorithmic, complex, yielded multiple solutions and involved nuanced judgment, interpretation, multiple criteria and uncertainty. Marzano et al. (1988) discussed five dimensions of thinking: (1) core thinking skills, including focusing, information-gathering, organizing and generating skills; (2) thinking processes, such as concept formation, problem solving and research; (3) critical and creative thinking; (4) the relationship of content-area knowledge to thinking; and (5) metacognition.

Further elaboration came from McGuinness (1999), who gave examples of different kinds of thinking: sequencing and ordering information, sorting, classifying and grouping; analyzing, identifying whole/part relationships, comparing and contrasting; making predictions and hypothesizing; drawing conclusions and giving reasons for conclusions; distinguishing fact from opinion; determining bias and checking the reliability of evidence; generating new ideas and brainstorming; relating cause and effect and designing a fair test; defining and clarifying problems, thinking up different solutions, setting up goals and subgoals; testing solutions and evaluating outcomes; planning and monitoring progress toward a goal and revising plans; making decisions, setting priorities, weighing pros and cons.

Critical thinking includes component skills of analyzing arguments, making inferences using inductive or deductive reasoning, judging or evaluating and making decisions or solving problems. Background knowledge is a necessary but not sufficient condition for critical thought. Critical thinking also involves dispositions, attitudes or habits of mind, including curiosity, flexibility, a propensity to seek reasons, a desire to be well-informed and a respect for and willingness to entertain diverse viewpoints. Teachers should teach how to transfer to new contexts, perhaps using cooperative or collaborative learning methods. Here the notions of "near" and "far" transfer become relevant. Assessment of critical thinking should use open-ended tasks, real-world or "authentic" problem contexts; problems that require students to go beyond recalling or restating learned information. Such tasks may have more than one defensible solution. Such assessment should make reasoning visible by requiring learners to provide evidence or logical arguments in support of judgments, choices, claims or assertions.

Of course, what is included in the definition can be somewhat arbitrary, depending on the age group, the context/subject matter and the degree of challenge. Other frameworks identify multiple intelligences, for example linguistic, logical, mathematical, musical, personal or kinesthetic intelligence. More recently, we have had suggested sub-divisions of "systems thinking" (Arnold & Wade, 2015), "computational thinking" in relation to computer programming (Moreno-León et al., 2019), "design thinking" (Tunga & Yildırım, 2017) and statistical thinking (Sharma, 2017).

We might summarize these multiple ideas in a table (Table 1.1):

TABLE 1.1
Aspects of the Definition of Thinking

Category	Activities
Focus and deploy standard thinking processes	focus attention, gather relevant information, retrieve and store memories, process information, abstraction, induction
Brainstorm: develop relevant ideas	problem definition, concept formation, connected ideas, questioning, assumptions, inferences
Sort ideas	analyze, sequence, order, sort, classify and group, logic, deduction, reasoning
Evaluate evidence	reflect, assess credibility, give evidence for and against, relate cause and effect, distinguish fact and opinion, speculate
Make conclusions	evaluate, judge, interpret, multiple criteria, draw conclusions
Propose solutions	select responses or actions, solve problems, think of different solutions, think of multiple solutions
Propose additional solutions	generate new ideas, creativity, set priorities, set goals

This gives us an approximate composite definition of thinking: focus and deploy standard thinking processes, brainstorm and develop relevant ideas, sort ideas, evaluate evidence, make conclusions, propose solutions and propose additional solutions.

Audience

The primary audience for this book is preservice and in-service teachers as well as teacher educators and individuals involved in supporting the ongoing professional development of educators, in elementary (primary) education and secondary (high) education. In addition, school principals and district superintendents and managers will seek to use the book as a reference source.

Officials in local and national government are also likely to use the book, as will researchers.

Why Read This Book?

The book is intended to give the evidence base for these programs in an easy and comprehensible way. This should reassure teachers and school/university managers that their practice is well substantiated. It also gives details of how each method can be implemented and refers readers to the original texts for more detail. Thus, readers are reassured that these methods work and are also given information about how to practically implement them in the classroom.

Structure of the Book

Generally, each chapter (apart from this first and the last two) follows the same model. A broad Introduction defines the method and introduces the originator(s) of the method. The effectiveness of the method is then summarized. Next comes a brief section about the theoretical underpinnings of the method. Then there is a substantial section on the structure of the method and how to implement it. This is followed by a section giving an example of the method in practice. A brief section on how to obtain training for the method follows, with a further brief section on how the method has been extended. References and a bibliography conclude the chapter, directing readers to the original texts for more detail if they wish.

The methods (chapters) are described in four sections: programs within particular traditional subjects, programs operable across the traditional curriculum, programs operating outside the traditional curriculum (which means special times have to be found for them) and programs that can operate either separately or within the curriculum (which includes more recent developments). This means that teachers heavily restricted by traditional curriculum requirements can still find ways described here to introduce thinking skills. The book concludes with a chapter on how to evaluate the development of thinking skills and finally a chapter which draws together the similar threads from the methods described, so readers have a useful summary of the main points of implementation.

Many books that claim to be evidence-based just give vague background research which is often not reflected in the recommendations they make, but in the case of this book, the research cited is specifically about the method described.

The book thus offers a summary of the independent, peer-reviewed research evidence on the methods described. This should address many of the major concerns of schools, who will have questions like: "Does it work?" "How should it be implemented to make it work?" and "Is it cheaper and more efficient in teacher time than what we were doing before?" This review of evidence should thus reassure schools that their practice is evidence-based and well substantiated, lead them to improve their implementation of such programs and enable them to state and defend their case in that regard to school district managers, local and national government, parents and other stakeholders. It will also be of interest to researchers, especially in areas where data are sparser or more difficult to track.

How to Read This Book

Each chapter is relatively brief and says more about how to do it than how effective it has been, so the book is not too long for the busy teacher to find time to read at least some of it. Read this Introduction first for an overview. After that, consider your context – how restricted are you in terms of the time available and the willingness of your hierarchy to allow some innovation? If neither of these are positive, you might need to avoid Section C "Programs Operating Outside the Traditional Curriculum", unless you have the fortitude and possibility to run these as an after-school club. Other sections lend themselves more to smuggling thinking skills into the classroom by disguising them as something else – but let's hope you don't need to do that. In any case, all readers will want to look at the last two chapters on implementation and similar features of programs.

Statistical Analysis

Some (but not many) statistics are present in what follows, so here is a brief overview. The *number* of observations is usually indicated as n or N (this is important in terms of the size and consequently significance of the study). The arithmetic *mean* or *average* is the sum of all observations divided by the number of observations. The *standard deviation* (s.d.) is a measure of the amount of variance in the data. In some analyses you will see that the difference between sets of observations is tested for statistical significance. One way of doing this is with the *t-test*, which compares the means with reference to their s.d.s and ns and sees if the value of the resulting statistic t is large enough to be statistically significant. Other ways are more complicated to explain.

Statistical significance is a quantification of whether what you see is likely just due to random chance or whether it is more probably the result of some influential factor you are studying. Usually, a criterion of probability of 0.05 or 5% is set as the limit of statistical significance, below which what you see is more likely due to your factor of interest, and above which is more likely due to random chance. Sometimes the sample size (n) for an analysis is very large, and one result of this is that even very small differences appear statistically significantly, as statistical significance is strongly affected by sample size – the larger the sample, the more likely statistical significance becomes.

An alternative way of looking at this is via *Effect Size* (ES) (a quantitative measure of the magnitude of effect). The larger the ES, the stronger the relationship between two variables. ESs are often approximately categorized according to their size: Very Small = 0.01, Small = 0.20, Medium = 0.50, Large = 0.80, Very Large = 1.20, Huge = 2.00. There is another kind of effect size (η^2) used occasionally, which we will talk about when it occurs.

Terminology

Bearing in mind differences in nomenclature and terms between the USA and the UK (among other countries), the book is written in transatlantic language, giving synonyms wherever appropriate (e.g., elementary/primary, students/pupils, mathematics not math or maths). Where single terms are used, the US version is usually given.

What Do Teachers Think About Thinking Skills?

There are a number of studies of teacher perceptions of thinking skills and training in the development thereof. Generally, they suggest that teachers have a vague perception that thinking skills are a good idea, but little idea about how to develop them. This is true irrespective of the country involved. Of course, that is why this book has been written. We will mention just one study here so as not to labor the point. Mullett et al. (2016) provided a review of empirical quantitative and qualitative investigations on this topic published in high quality journals from 1999 to 2015. Although teachers valued creative thinking, their conceptions were uninformed by theory and research. They felt unprepared to foster or identify creative thinking in their classrooms and equated it with the arts.

Overviews of Thinking Skills Effectiveness

In this section we will look at exemplary research reviews of thinking skills, to answer the general question: Does teaching thinking skills work? As long ago as 1990, Bangert-Drowns and Bankert produced a meta-analysis of thinking skills programs. Examining 250 control group studies from ERIC and Dissertation Abstracts International and selecting 20 as suitable for the meta-analysis, 19 of which were doctoral dissertations, these authors distinguished programs that taught critical thinking in a subject matter domain from those that taught CT generally. All used a general measure of critical thinking as the final criteria. Ten used the Watson-Glaser Critical Thinking Appraisal and five used the Cornell Critical Thinking Test. Findings from 18 of the 20 studies favored critical thinking instruction, eight significantly. Only two studies produced negative findings, and these were non-significant.

The average effect size was 0.37, equivalent to increasing student performance from the 50th to the 64th percentile. Students in younger grades benefited more from critical thinking instruction than did students in high school and college. The average effect size for elementary and junior high grades was 0.50, for high school and college 0.21. Interestingly, there was no evidence that length of treatment was related to the effects of treatment. Infusion approaches were embedded in a subject, while general approaches were taught separately. Infusion programs did no better than separate programs. Results consistently favored programs that used explicit instruction methods. Intensive programs proved more effective than did programs providing only periodic training.

More recently, Taggart et al. (2005) reviewed thinking skills teaching in the early years and reported that discrete approaches included: Philosophy for Children, Cognitive Acceleration Through Science Education and Paired Thinking (all of which have their own chapters later in this book). Approaches infused into normal curricular subjects tended to draw on a broader range of subjects and a broader variety of activity, that is, drama and role-play. The conclusion was that compared to infused approaches, discrete approaches to thinking skills appeared to allow children to develop their abilities more systematically.

Also in 2005, Higgins et al. (2005) reported a meta-analysis of the impact of thinking skills teaching on school students. Twenty-nine studies contained quantitative data on pupils' attainment and attitudes in both primary and secondary schools. Instrumental Enrichment and Cognitive Acceleration through Science Education were mentioned, as well as studies reporting a more general thinking skills approach. Thinking skills programs were effective in improving performance on tests of cognitive measures, with an overall effect size of 0.62 (moderate to large).

There was also a considerable impact on curricular outcomes, with the same effect size of 0.62. The overall effect size (including cognitive, curricular and affective measures) was 0.74. Instrumental Enrichment had moderate overall effects (Effect Size – ES = 0.43 on reasoning ability). There was some indication that impact might vary according to subject – there was relatively greater impact on tests of mathematics (0.89) and science (0.78), compared with reading (0.40).

Baumfield et al. (2005) considered the effect of teaching thinking skills on teachers, synthesizing 13 studies. This resulted in changes in pedagogical practice, including teacher questioning/grouping of pupils/changes in planning and assessment and changes in attitudes toward pupils, and including different perceptions of pupil abilities/facilitation of greater pupil responsibility and autonomy/access to pupil learning.

In 2008, Abrami et al. conducted a meta-analysis on critical thinking skills and dispositions, analyzing 117 studies yielding 161 effect sizes, with an average effect size of 0.34. The studies were extremely varied. Effect Sizes were higher for elementary (0.52) and secondary (0.69) education, but lower for upper high school (0.10) and undergraduate education (0.25). Abrami et al. (2008) compared infusion and general approaches with mixed and subject "immersion" programs (where critical thinking principles are not made explicit). Mixed interventions produced the highest effect size (0.94), followed by infusion approaches (0.54), general programs (0.38) and immersion programs (0.09). Training was an important factor in effectiveness. Student collaboration yielded higher effect sizes.

Abrami et al. (2015) updated their meta-analysis to include 341 effect sizes and found a mean of 0.30, again with heterogeneity. This effect size excluded various outlier results, so is more conservative than the 2008 figure. Again, elementary and middle school pupils did best (ES = 0.37), upper high school and undergraduates less well (0.25). Immersion approaches did better in this study, but still had the lowest effect size. As might be expected, specific critical thinking skills increased more than general achievement. The opportunity for dialogue, the exposure of students to situated problems and examples and mentoring had positive effects on critical thinking skills.

A focus on post-secondary education characterized the work of Behar and Niu (2011), who reviewed 42 empirical studies. "Immersion" methods were the least effective. Length of intervention was very various. Just over half the outcomes were statistically significant with shorter programs, but with longer intervention lengths 70% were significant. The results suggested that implementation quality was important if results were to be good. Qualitative data was important to supplement quantitative data, since in small studies statistical significance could be misleading. The systematic literature review of Hamzah et al. (2022) used only two databases and extracted 15 articles, focusing again on schools. Of these, 11 unequivocally showed improvement as a result of critical thinking teaching. However, cognitive skills were not widely practiced outside of the intervention context.

Overall, then, teaching critical thinking seems to be effective in most studies. Effectiveness might vary by context of subject. Implementation quality and length of intervention cause some variation, and there is little evidence on long-term follow-up and generalization beyond the thinking context. Thinking skills teaching changes teachers as well as students.

What This Book Is Not

The approaches mentioned in the chapters that follow have been found to be effective, and the research on them is briefly summarized. However, there are many other thinking programs that have not been widely evaluated or not evaluated at all. These include: The Structure of Intellect, Science – a Process Approach, Think About, Patterns of Problem-Solving, A Practicum of Thinking, The Cognitive Studies Project, The Productive Thinking Program, ADAPT (Accent on the Development of Abstract Processes of Thought), DOORS (Development of Operational Reasoning Skills), COMPAS (Consortium for Operating and Managing Programs for the Advancement of Skills), SOAR (Stress on Analytical Reasoning), DORIS (Development of Reasoning in Science), LOGO and Procedural Thinking and many others. We do not further mention these approaches in this book.

Now we will turn to the major chapters in this book, which examine individual approaches more carefully and spell out the implementation issues, starting with programs which are embedded in particular subjects.

References and Bibliography

Abrami, P. C., Bernard, R. M., Borokhovski, E., Waddington, D. I., Wade, C. A., & Persson, T. (2015). Strategies for teaching students to think critically: A meta-analysis. *Review of Educational Research*, *85*(2), 275–314. https://doi.org/10.3102/003465431455106

Abrami, P. C., Bernard, R. M., Borokhovski, E., Wade, A., Surkes, M. A., Tamim, R., & Zhang, D. (2008). Instructional interventions affecting critical thinking skills and dispositions: A stage 1 meta-analysis. *Review of Educational Research*, *78*(4), 1102–1134. https://doi.org/10.3102/0034654308326084

Arnold, R. D., & Wade, J. P. (2015). A definition of systems thinking: A systems approach. *Procedia Computer Science*, *44*, 669–678. https://doi.org/10.1016/j.procs.2015.03.050

Bangert-Drowns, R. L., & Bankert, E. (1990). *Meta-analysis of effects of explicit instruction for critical thinking*. Paper presented at *the Annual Meeting of the American Educational Research Association* (Boston, MA, April 16–20, 1990). ERIC number ED 328 614.

Baumfield, V. M., Butterworth, M., & Edwards, G. (2005). The impact of the implementation of thinking skills programmes and approaches on teachers. In *Research evidence in education library*. London: EPPI-Centre, Social Science Research Unit, Institute of Education, University of London.

Behar-Horenstein, L. S., & Niu, L. (2011). Teaching critical thinking skills in higher education: A review of the literature. *Journal of College Teaching & Learning*, 8(2), 25–41. https://doi.org/10.19030/tlc.v8i2.3554

Hamzah, H., Hamzah, M.I., & Zulkifli, H. (2022). Systematic literature review on the elements of metacognition-based higher order thinking skills (HOTS) teaching and learning modules. *Sustainability*, *14*, 813. https://doi.org/10.3390/su14020813

Higgins, S., Hall, E., Baumfield, V., & Moseley, D. (2005). A meta-analysis of the impact of the implementation of thinking skills approaches on pupils. In *Research evidence in education library*. London: EPPI-Centre, Social Science Research Unit, Institute of Education, University of London. https://dro.dur.ac.uk/1890/

Marzano, R. J., Brandt, R. S., Hughes, C. S., Jones, B. F., Presseisen, B. Z., Rankin, S. C., & Suhor, C. (1988). *Dimensions of thinking: A framework for curriculum and instruction*. Alexandria, VA: The Association for Supervision and Curriculum Development. ERIC number ED 294 222.

McGuinness, C. (1999). *From thinking skills to thinking classrooms: A review and evaluation of approaches for developing pupils' thinking*. DfEE Research Report No 115. Norwich: HMSO. https://doi.org/10.13140/RG.2.1.4000.1129

Moreno-León, J., Robles, G., Román-González, M., & García, J. D. R. (2019). Not the same: A text network analysis on computational thinking definitions to study its relationship with computer programming. *Revista Interuniversitaria de Investigación en Tecnología Educativa (RIITE)*, 7, 26–35. https://doi.org/10.6018/riite.397151

Mullet, D. R., Willerson, A., Lamb, K. N., & Kettler, T. (2016). Examining teacher perceptions of creativity: A systematic review of the literature. *Thinking Skills and Creativity*, *21*, 9–30. https://doi.org/10.1016/j.tsc.2016.05.001

Presseisen, B. Z. (1986). *Critical thinking and thinking skills: State of the art definitions and practice in public schools*. Washington, DC: Research for Better Schools, Office of Educational Research and Improvement.

Sharma, S. (2017). Definitions and models of statistical literacy: A literature review. *Open Review of Educational Research*, *4*(1), 118–133. https://doi.org/10.1080/23265507.2017.1354313

Taggart, G., Ridley, K., Rudd, P., & Benefield, P. (2005). *Thinking skills in the early years: A literature review*. Research Report. Slough: National Foundation for Educational Research. Available: https://eprints.whiterose.ac.uk/73999/

Tunga, Y., & Yildirim, S. (2017). Revisiting design thinking: A review of definitions and implications. *Ege Eğitim Teknolojileri Dergisi*, *1*(1), 92–102. Retrieved from https://dergipark.org.tr/en/pub/eetd/issue/29867/300287

Section A

Programs Within a Traditional Subject

These programs should not be overlooked by teachers of subjects other than science, mathematics and reading, because all of them have elements that are relevant to other subjects, and indeed some of them have already been widely applied (e.g., CASE also to mathematics, English and other subjects).

2

Science

Cognitive Acceleration Through Science Education (CASE)

CASE is largely associated with the work of Michael Shayer and Philip Adey. They developed their program to improve children's thinking in the course of science education, utilizing a series of 30 worksheets that posed thinking problems in areas of science where formal operational thinking (in Piaget's terms) was needed. This was spread from elementary/primary schools to secondary/high schools, and then to mathematics as well as science and then to other subjects.

Effects of CASE

The first CASE teaching materials were written for early secondary school science lessons. The original CASE experiment was conducted with an experimental/control pre-test, post-test and delayed post-test design. After three years, the results of intervening in science teaching in a dozen classes were compared with control classes, which were taught in the usual way. The findings showed both immediate and long term accelerated cognitive development. Most impressive of the results was that three years after the end of the intervention, participating students showed improvements in their GCSE (the UK General Certificate of Secondary Education) grades, not only in science but also in mathematics and English.

The original experiment included only a small number of students (approximately 130 students in the experimental and control groups), but subsequent experiments with successive cohorts of schools since the 1990s included over 2,000 students from 11 schools and gave similar findings. It is rare to see such transfer of learning to other subjects in educational research, and also rare to see follow-up over time, which showed sustained gains. Adey and Shayer (1990) argued that the fundamental way the participating students processed information had changed – they had gained long term access to ways of thinking that had impacted their learning across the curriculum.

Equally, discourse and interaction between students while engaged in CASE activities changed. Venville et al. (2003) conducted a multiple case study of 32 lessons, of which four were analyzed in detail. The authors found that students participating in CASE thinking lessons for Year 1 (5- and 6-year-old students) compared with regular curriculum lessons on a similar subject were more frequently involved in: explaining their ideas and other students' ideas; highlighting discrepancies between group members' ideas; adopting or changing their own ideas when a better idea was presented by another group member; making suggestions for solving problems; and building on other students' ideas. The results indicated that teachers could foster habits of good thinking through science: first, by accepting difficulty as an integral part of the learning process; second, by encouraging children to explain and talk about their ideas and, finally, by creating an environment where thinking was a valued classroom process.

Since then, there have been studies from many parts of the world that have all tended to show the same picture.

Theoretical Underpinnings of CASE

CASE relies heavily on the notion of formal operations derived from Piaget (however, it roundly rejects Piaget's assertion that cognition is not modifiable). The reasoning patterns of formal operations can be grouped thus:

- Handling Variables: control and exclusion of variables, classifications
- Relationships between Variables: ratio and proportionality, compensation and equilibrium, correlation, probability
- Formal Models: constructing and using formal models, logical reasoning

Regarding these, in their naïve explanations, students typically change more than one variable, or include variables that are not relevant, and they need a process that enables them to test one variable at a time. Beyond this, variables can be categorized, but students need to see that categorization can be carried out according to multiple criteria. Determining the relevant criteria is important.

Ratio describes a *constant* multiplicative relationship between two variables, and proportionality is the comparison of two ratios. Compensation is the opposite of ratio – as one variable goes up, the other declines. Equilibrium (or reciprocity) involves the equating of two compensations, as with a scale on which weights of different amounts can be moved different distances on each side to achieve the same balance. Correlation estimates the amount of effect that might be attributed to any particular cause but cannot prove causal relationships. Probability indicates the degree to which certainty can be attributed to conclusions. More examples than one are required to indicate whether the result stems from random chance or from a causal effect of a variable, that is, arguing from a sample of one is very weak argument.

A model is a representation of something else. Formal models involve abstract entities that have to be imagined. Logical reasoning involves analyzing the combinatorial relationships present in the information given to determine what causes what. This is perhaps the trickiest part of the process for students.

Adey and Shayer (1994) showed that the capability of students to deal with formal operations lagged well behind the requirements of the science curriculum. In other words, students did not have the thinking tools to understand and deal with the activities they were required to undertake.

Consequently, various thinking tools were used in the program. The first was "cognitive conflict" – which stemmed from contact with a concept or event that students found puzzling or disconcerting, perhaps because it clashed with previous opinions. The teacher needs to expose the conceptions the students hold before teaching. The second was the "Construction Zone" – whereby in interaction with the teacher or other students, old understandings were reframed and new (and more complex) understandings developed. The third was "Bridging" – deliberately generalizing a concept to new contexts and determining what needs to change as a result.

Structure and Implementation of CASE

The CASE curricular materials are known as Thinking Science and consist of 30 activities that consecutively target aspects of formal operational thinking (Adey, Shayer, & Yates, 1989). Early activities focus on control and exclusion of variables and then progress to proportionality, probability, correlation, compensation, formal models and so forth. Each activity has specific examples given and is accompanied by teacher and pupil worksheets. Thinking Science was designed to be taught over two years to 11–12-year-olds (first year of secondary school) but has since been used with higher grades.

Concrete preparation involved the teacher establishing the nature of the activity, the associated vocabulary and the problem for the students to consider. During concrete preparation, the teacher and students negotiated any ideas associated with the lesson. Lessons were constructed around reasoning patterns (or schemata), including controlling variables, ratio and proportionality, compensation and equilibrium to analyze process, using correlation, probability, classification, formal models of thinking and compound variables. The Vygotskian idea of a Zone of Proximal Development (ZPD) was relevant – cognition was stimulated by the presentation of intellectual challenges of moderate difficulty that must be accompanied by support (or scaffolding) to discuss, question, suggest and problem solve (Oliver, Venville, & Adey, 2012).

Teachers sought to maximize cognitive conflict (a Piagetian notion) in the early stages of problem solving, that is, offer learning experiences which were discordant or puzzling for the students' current level of understanding. Students may report "this doesn't make sense" and this was the driver of cognitive development, as students needed to discuss the problem or data or develop an explanation. This social construction occurred as students worked together in groups, sharing the development of explanations and understandings. The lesson activities contained questions on the worksheets that students worked through, which arose from each activity and directly targeted explanations.

Teachers played a key role in establishing good group work, encouraging students to think about and consider a range of possible explanations for the problem. During this stage, the teacher's role was to listen to the discussion in each group, without interacting with them except to ask a prompting question, such as "See if you can find a pattern in the data you have collected", "What that might tell you?" or "How could you explain those results?" CASE progresses from concrete materials to abstract generalizations and to do this the student must develop a vocabulary for talking about thinking.

The metacognition stage of each lesson enabled students to articulate and "hear" each other's solutions to the problem solving and reasoning, and once again this depended on the skills of the teacher to stimulate and give time for this sort of thinking. For teachers inexperienced in these lessons, it might have felt rather laborious, probing students and asking them for their ideas and explanations, but this was considered essential as all students contributed their group's ideas to the general discussion. Skillful teachers, having heard pivotal ideas emerge in the construction phase of the lesson, would be able to judiciously select students or groups to respond to questions in this phase, to elicit answers to the questions from the most concrete to the more sophisticated levels of thinking.

In this way, not only were all students' ideas welcomed, shared and heard, but they were also all able to hear how different answers and explanations varied with different levels of thinking and their own thinking could be clarified or modified. CASE helped students to make their thought patterns explicit by reflecting on, explaining and evaluating their problem-solving strategies. Finally, bridging involved applying the ideas developed to other problems in normal science lessons or the real world. CASE made extensive use of bridging,to promote the transfer of a skill learned in one context to a new context.

Examples of CASE Activities

The 30 CASE activities are listed in Table 2.1:

Activity number 1 is called Variables and is based on seeking relationships between variables in simple situations such as figures varying in terms of shape, size and coloration. Students discover different sorts of relationships and also generate examples where no such relationships exist.

Activity number 3 is called Tubes. Students are given a number of tubes of varying length and diameter and material, and they have to find out what factors affect the note made when the end of the tube is blown across. They are encouraged to test the tubes in pairs. As soon as a hypothesis develops, students are asked to report it to the teacher – maybe diameter makes a difference. The teacher asks the student(s) to show the principle in action, but maybe the student blows across two tubes that are of different diameters but also of different lengths. Simply comparing any two tubes does not produce the right answer. The student is encouraged to try again and compare findings and discuss with other students.

Activity number 5 is called Rollerball, and uses balls of various masses, materials and sizes on a curved track which rises to a height at one end and rises slightly at the other end. A target ball is placed at a marked spot on the relatively level part of the track and a rollerball dropped from a height that is recorded. The dropped ball impacts the stationary ball and pushes it along the track, the distance again being recorded. This could be repeated

TABLE 2.1
Case Activities

No.	Activity	Formal Schema
1	What varies?	Variables
2	Two variables	Variables
3	Tubes – the "fair" test	Variables
4	What sort of relationship?	Variables
5	Roller ball	Variables
6	Gears and ratios	Proportionality
7	Scaling: pictures and microscopes	Proportionality
7a	Bean growth 1	Probability
7b	Bean growth 2	Probability
8	The wheelbarrow	Proportionality
9	Trunks and twigs	Compensation
10	The balance beam	Compensation
11	Current, length and thickness	Compensation
12	Volts, amps and watts	Compensation
13	Spinning coins	Probability
14	Combinations	Combinations
15	Tea tasting	Probability
16	Interaction	Variables
17	The behavior of woodlice	Correlation
18	Treatments and effects	Correlation
19	Sampling: fish in a pond	Probability
20	Throwing dice	Probability
21	Making groups	Classification
22	Classifying birds	Classification
23	Explaining states of matter	Formal Models
24	Explaining solutions	Formal Models
25	Explaining chemical reactions	Formal Models
26	Pressure	Compound Variables
27	Floating and sinking	Compound Variables
28	Up hill and down dale	Equilibrium
29	Equilibrium in the balance	Equilibrium
30	Divers	Compound Variables

with balls of different masses and sizes dropped from different heights onto target balls located in different positions on the track.

Activity number 8 is called Wheelbarrow and explores proportionality. Students have a "wheelbarrow" which is just a notched stick, with one end propped on a table and the other end attached vertically to a force meter. A load is added to a notch on the stick, and then loads of successively increasing weight are hung from other notches, and students record the relationship between weight and amount of force exerted. When they have about six observations, they draw a graph to relate load to force of lift (which should be a straight line, of course). From this they are asked to make predictions about what the force would be with extra loads that are not available to them. The first predictions can be estimated by extrapolation of the graph, but then the graph paper runs out. Now a more sophisticated view of the relationship, involving a constant ratio of load to effort, has to be evolved. This abstract mathematical model shows strikingly how to proceed from the concrete to the abstract.

Activity number 21 is called Classification and explores classification into groups. There is a set of six related exercises that involve sorting entities into groups according to criteria that the students themselves develop. Examples would be: animals, foodstuffs, chemicals by color and solubility. Then the students are asked to consider their classifications and say which was the most difficult or raised the most conflict, and which was the easiest and why. They compare their feelings with other groups and discuss why some groups found it difficult and some easy. Students were thus encouraged to reflect upon their own thinking strategies, and by articulating them, they clarify what they mean and increase the likelihood of remembering them.

Of course, these activities are only sample activities, and teachers are encouraged to devise their own activities that echo some of the principles involved.

Training for CASE

Joyce and Showers (1988) noted that an in-service program should contain several elements: the provision of *information* and theory, a *demonstration* of the method by the trainers, an opportunity for participants to *practice* the new method, provision of *feedback* to participants on their practice and *coaching* of participants in their own school setting. This information → demonstration → practice → feedback → coaching cycle was embodied in the CASE continuing professional development program.

Over the two-year program of CASE, for example, teachers were provided with six days away from school to participate in professional development associated with the preparation, implementation and evaluation of the program. Time was given to teachers for classroom coaching and participating teachers had a sense of ownership and commitment. The extensive professional development over the period of the intervention provided for teacher learning, reflection and planning.

Extensions of CASE

Using a similar approach to teaching elementary/primary and secondary/high mathematics (CAME) produced similar results (Shayer & Adhami, 2010). Later development extended the range of lesson activities in elementary/primary science to the lower grades (1–4, ages 4–10). Then came the development of activities for technology (Backwell & Hamaker, 2004) and the arts (Gouge & Yates, 2002). These all followed the same Piagetian principles of developing formal operations, but all rejected the Piagetian notion of non-modifiability of cognitive status. Cognitive acceleration programs also have been successfully adapted and trialed in other places in the world including China, Malawi, Finland, Oregon (USA), Pakistan and Australia. Even a short intervention using abbreviated CASE materials in Israel was effective.

References and Bibliography

Adey, P., Robertson, A., & Venville, G. (2002). Effects of a cognitive acceleration programme on Year 1 pupils. *British Journal of Educational Psychology, 72*, 1–25. https://doi.org/10.1348/000709902158748

Adey, P., & Shayer, M. (1990). Accelerating the development of formal thinking in middle and high-school students. *Journal of Research in Science Teaching, 27,* 267–285. https://doi.org/10.1002/tea.3660270309

Adey, P., & Shayer, M. (1994). *Really raising standards: Cognitive intervention and academic achievement.* London & New York: Routledge.

Adey, P. S., Shayer, M., & Yates, C. (1989). *Thinking science: The curriculum materials of the CASE project.* London: Macmillan.

Backwell, J. L., & Hamaker, A. (2004). The design and development of Cognitive Acceleration through Technology Education (CATE): Implications for teacher education. *Trends in Technology Education Research, 30,* 55–56. epiSTEME - 1 conference, Dona Paula, Goa, India. December 13–17, 2004. https://www.law.uwa.edu.au/__data/assets/pdf_file/0016/1025026/CATE_implications_for_teacher_education_.pdf

Gouge, K., & Yates, C. (2002). Creating a cognitive acceleration programme in the arts: The Wigan LEA arts project. In Shayer, M., & Adey, P. (Ed.), *Learning intelligence: Cognitive acceleration across the curriculum from 5 to 15 years.* Maidenhead: Open University Press.

Higgins, S., Hall, E., Baumfield, V., & Moseley, D. (2005). A meta-analysis of the impact of the implementation of thinking skills approaches on pupils. In *Research evidence in education library.* London: EPPI-Centre, Social Science Research Unit, Institute of Education, University of London. https://dro.dur.ac.uk/1890/

Joyce, B., & Showers, B. (1988). *Student achievement through staff development.* New York: Longman.

Oliver, M., Venville, G., & Adey, P. (2012). Effects of a cognitive acceleration programme in a low socioeconomic high school in regional Australia. *International Journal of Science Education, 34*(9), 1393–1410. https://doi.org/10.1080/09500693.2012.673241

Shayer, M., & Adey, P. S. (1993). Accelerating the development of formal thinking in middle and high school students: Three years after a two-year intervention. *Journal of Research in Science Teaching, 30*(4), 351–366. https://doi.org/10.1002/tea.3660300404

Shayer, M., & Adhami, M. (2010). Realizing the cognitive potential of children 5–7 with a mathematics focus: Post-test and long-term effects of a 2-year intervention. *British Journal of Educational Psychology*, *80*(3), 363–379. https://doi.org/10.1348/000709909X482363

Venville, G., Adey, P., Larkin, S., Robertson, A., & Fulham, H. (2003). Fostering thinking through science in the early years of schooling. *International Journal of Science Education*, *25*(11), 1313–1331. https://doi.org/10.1080/0950069032000052090

3

Mathematics

Cognitively Guided Instruction in Mathematics (CGI)

CGI is understanding how children think mathematically, in order to develop a sequence of problems and structures in mathematics classes that position students to see themselves as competent problem solvers and support them to engage in each other's ideas, so that they can build on their understanding of the underlying ideas of mathematics. CGI is student-centered and builds on children's intuitive ideas for solving mathematical problems or tasks. The primary role of the teacher is that of an organizer of problems, listener, facilitator and strategic questioner.

CGI was started by Thomas Carpenter and Elizabeth Fennema as a research program to investigate the impact of research-based knowledge about children's thinking on teachers and their students (Carpenter et al., 1999). (The second edition of this book includes extensive online video, Carpenter et al., 2015). As CGI does not have any mathematical content, it has often been regarded as a professional development (PD) program rather than an intervention in itself. The PD program focuses on teachers' knowledge and beliefs that influence their instructional practices. Although teachers have a great deal of intuitive knowledge about children's mathematical thinking, it is fragmented and generally does not play an important role in most teachers' decision-making.

Children intuitively solve word problems by modeling the action and relations described in them. Basic concepts of addition, subtraction, multiplication and division develop naturally in children and they can construct concepts of place value and multidigit computational procedures based on their intuitive mathematical knowledge. In CGI classrooms students spend most of their time solving problems. Various physical materials are available to children to assist them in solving the problems. Each child decides how and when to use the materials, fingers, paper and pencil; or to solve the problem mentally. The teacher and peers listen and question until they understand.

Effects of CGI

In the initial experimental study (Carpenter et al. 1989), the authors found that CGI classes had significantly higher levels of achievement in problem solving than control classes. Although there was significantly less emphasis on number skills in CGI classes, there was no difference between the groups in achievement on the test of number skills. In fact, there was some evidence that CGI students actually had better recall of number facts than did students in the control classes. Additionally, a standardized achievement test, which also measured computation skills, was administered in this study and no differences were found between CGI and control classes.

In a related study using the same measures, Villasenor and Kepner (1993) had 12 first-grade teachers in a CGI staff development, with another group of 12 making up a comparison group. The percentage of minority students ranged from 57% to 99%. Teachers in the experimental group taught arithmetic through the use of word problems and their students spent considerably less time on skill worksheet drills. Students in experimental classes performed significantly better in solving word problems as well as completing number facts.

Carpenter et al. (1993) interviewed 70 kindergarten children as they solved addition, subtraction, multiplication, division, multistep and nonroutine word problems. Thirty-two children used a valid strategy for all nine problems and 44 correctly answered seven or more problems. Only five children were not able to answer any problems correctly. The results suggest that children could solve a wide range of problems, including problems involving multiplication and division situations, much earlier than had generally been presumed. Many teachers considered the problems too difficult for young children, but the study results provided compelling evidence that children as young as kindergarten could invent strategies to solve a variety of problems if they were given the opportunity to do so. With only a few exceptions, children's strategies could be characterized as representing or modeling the action or relationships described in the problems. Modeling offered a parsimonious and coherent way of thinking about children's mathematical problem solving that was relatively straightforward and accessible to teachers and students alike.

However, the largest and most through evaluations were done by Schoen and colleagues in Florida. In 2018, Schoen et al. reported the effects of a CGI PD program for teachers in grades 3–5, consisting of five consecutive seven-hour days during summer; two consecutive six-hour days in fall; and two consecutive days six-hour days in winter. One hundred forty-nine teachers representing 32 schools voluntarily participated. Teachers were then assigned at random to the intervention group or the wait-list comparison group. Comparison group teachers participated in business-as-usual professional development and mathematics instruction. Student achievement was measured by the Elementary Mathematics Student Assessment (EMSA), not by a problem-solving test – designed to assess student achievement in understanding fraction quantities and operations involving whole numbers and fractions.

A treatment effect of Effect Size = 0.18 (p = .007) was found, with no statistically significant interactions between treatment and grade level or treatment and baseline achievement scores. The effect size of the PD program on student achievement was greater than many of the most effective teacher professional-development programs that have been subjected to rigorous evaluation.

Later, Schoen et al. (2022) studied the impact of a long-term teacher professional development program on elementary school mathematics achievement five years after the initial randomization, using data for kindergarten through fifth-grade students. Teachers from 22 schools participated. The intervention had a small positive effect (effect size = 0.03) on mathematics achievement in K1–2 and a larger effect size (0.16) in grades 3–5. However, an effect size of 0.03 is equivalent to the average effect-size estimate of all mathematics interventions studied in randomized controlled trials funded by the US Department of Education. Grade level was the only statistically significant moderator, with larger effects in higher grade levels. These results yielded evidence of a long-term effect of CGI on student learning in mathematics. It is possible, therefore, that effects on students could materialize after the researchers stopped looking for them.

There are many other studies of CGI, usually with smaller samples and a focus on a limited number of grades.

Theoretical Underpinnings of CGI

CGI has a simple theory, which is that students have natural and informal ways of solving problems and the teacher's task is to understand this and promote it. CGI capitalizes on children's natural problem-solving skills by allowing students to practice multiple strategies when solving one problem. Eventually, students develop their paths to the solution. CGI grants the student autonomy and power to guide the learning method. Students analyze the various options available and apply previously acquired knowledge to find a resolution, which makes them very effective at solving mathematical problems on their own. The teacher then uses the information from the observation to help the students understand how they identify the solution to the problem.

Symbols are learned not as abstractions but as a way of representing situations that children already understand. Rather than expecting children to learn skills in isolation and then learn how to apply those skills to solve problems, the learning of computational procedures is facilitated by problem-solving experiences that permit children to invent ways to calculate answers to problems. The thesis of CGI is thus that children have experiential knowledge and informal knowledge of mathematics that can serve as the basis for developing a more formal understanding of the elementary mathematics curriculum.

Children can build on their intuitive knowledge to develop a progressively abstract understanding of and formalized strategies for addition, subtraction, multiplication and division with single-digit whole numbers, multi-digit whole numbers and fractions, as well as the base-ten number system and fractions concepts. A CGI approach to teaching is mindful that children often view mathematics differently than adults do and that striving to understand the child's perspective is an important part of teaching. Within this conceptual framework, a teacher's role is to design and implement instruction in a way that leverages and elevates children's ways of knowing and understanding such that they are used as a foundation for building new knowledge.

CGI PD conceptualizes teaching as a problem-solving endeavor, in which teachers can use information gained by attending to the mathematical thinking of their students to further refine their knowledge of children's thinking and how instruction can be designed to support its further development. CGI teachers learn to select or create mathematical tasks that expose student thinking in relation to various learning goals, and they become increasingly adept at being responsive to student understanding and using students' ideas to support student learning.

Effects on teachers, teaching and students occur through an iterative process over an extended period, both within and across school years and over an extended duration of formal and informal experiences. Participating teachers play an active role in creating coherence between their daily work and the ideas they encounter in CGI PD. This dynamic allows for the changes in knowledge and beliefs that may occur through participation in the workshops to transfer into long-term, significant changes in instructional practice.

Structure and Implementation of CGI

Basic Word Problem Types: The word problem types are focused on the arithmetic operations, which are addition, subtraction, multiplication and division. The types of mathematical word problems for addition and subtraction are broken down into four basic categories, which are: join problems, separate problems, part-part-whole problems and compare problems.

Join Problems: Join problems involve a direct or implied action of increasing a set by a particular amount over time, fundamentally presented as an addition problem. Each join word problem has three components. Those components are the Start, Change, and Result. There are three classifications of join problems. Join, Result Unknown problems occur when the result is the unknown part of the word problem. The starting point of the problem and the additional changing factor of the problem are known. Join, Change Unknown problems have the starting factor and the result of the problem as known components, but the changing factor in the word problem is unknown. Join, Start Unknown problems occur when the starting number of the problem is known; however, the word problem contains the result and the changing factors of the problem.

Separate Problems: Separate problems are only different from Join problems in the notion that they are presented as subtraction problems. The separate problems have a direct or implied action of decreasing a set of numbers by a particular amount over time. Every separate word problem has three components, which are Start, Change and Result. Separate problems also have three classifications similar to Join problems. Separate, Result Unknown problems are presented as word problems where the result of the situation is unknown but the starting factor and changing factor are known. Separate, Change Unknown problems lack the change factor but contain the starting factor and result of the word problem. Separate, Start Unknown problems are the problems where the starting factor of the situation is unknown but the word problem has the changing factor and the resulting factor.

Part-Part-Whole Problems: Part-part-whole problems are somewhat different from Join and Separate problems. Part-part-whole problems have no change over time, do not have a direct or implied action and the factors are not exactly the same categories, that is, a whole of soccer players with a part of male soccer players and a part of female soccer players. In other words, part-part-whole problems involve a fixed relationship between one larger group and two similar but slightly different subgroups. Since the part factors are considered to do the same task, there are only two distinctions for problem types. Part-Part-Whole, Whole Unknown problems have the two-part factors known but the resultant whole factor unknown. The Part-Part-Whole, Part Unknown word problem has one of the part factors as unknown but the other part factor and the whole factor are known.

Compare Problems: Compare problems are the final category of problem types for addition and subtraction problems. Compare problems are similar to part-part-whole problems because they both have relationships between different groups as the focus of their distinction. As the title of this category suggests, compare problems have a comparison relationship between three number groups, which are also known as the components of a compare problem. The three components are the Referent, the Compared Quantity and the Difference.

Corresponding with the three components of a compare problem, there are three compare problem types. Compare, Difference Unknown problems have the difference unknown while the referent and the compared quantity are known. A Compare, Compared Quantity Unknown word problem has the referent set and difference present in the problem, but the compared quantity is unknown. The Compare, Referent Unknown problems have the compared set and the difference known in the word problem but not the referent.

Multiplication and Division Problems: The essential components of multiplication and division word problems can be described by one basic problem type, while addition and subtraction word problems have four basic problem types. This basic problem type involves the assumption that the word problem can be grouped or partitioned into equal groups and does not have a remainder. That assumption is made to simplify the explanation of multiplication and division problems. In addition, children tend to view and solve most possible manifestations of multiplication and division problems in the three different forms of the basic problem types.

The one basic multiplication and division word problem type can be used as three different problem types. Those problem types are Multiplication, Measurement Division and Partitive Division. Basic multiplication and division problems have the three components of the number of groups, number of items per group and the total number of items.

Similar to the addition and subtraction problems, the difference between the three multiplication and division problem types is based on the unknown component in the problem. Multiplication word problems have the total number of items as the unknown factor, while the number of groups and number of items per group are known. Measurement Division problems have the number of items per group and the total number of items known, but the number of groups is unknown. Partitive Division problems have the number of items per group as the unknown. The number of groups and the total number of items are known in Partitive Division word problems.

Remainders: Multiplication and division word problems can be fashioned to have remainders. Problems with remainders are generally not much more difficult for children than multiplication and division problems that have equal groups and no remainder. When children begin working with multiplication and division problems that have remainders, the possible meaning of a remainder should be explored with the children to ensure that they understand what a remainder means in different scenarios.

Number of Digits: Teachers have two basic considerations when creating an arithmetic word problem for their students. First, the teacher must consider which problem type is most suited for the current instructional goals. For example, the teacher must figure if a Join, Result Unknown problem or a Compare, Difference Unknown problem is more suitable for mathematics instruction. Second, the teacher considers how small or large the numbers are that will be used with the chosen word problem type. The type of the word problem and the number of digits in the word problem are the two basic elements that affect the complexity and difficulty of the word problem.

When children approach these more difficult, multidigit problems, they tend to use algorithms. Those can be standard algorithms or invented algorithms. Invented algorithms allow students to practice and learn different ways of problem solving within mathematics. Invented algorithms represent a developed sense of abstract thought for mathematics; however, standard algorithms that are known to a person represent the most abstract and efficient way to solve particular multidigit problems.

Solution Strategies: There are various solution strategies for the different arithmetic word problems previously discussed. The solution strategies have also been broken down into three categories of distinguishable strategies of modeling, and the categories are Direct Modeling, Counting and Number Facts/Algorithms. It may be easiest to picture the solutions strategies as forms of modeling that originate as very concrete, physical forms of modeling, then become mentally based forms of modeling and eventually are solid mental concepts of number facts and their relationships in formal procedures. It is important to understand the different problem types because children tend to view and work with each kind of the word problem types in important and different ways. Some solution strategies are more appropriate and common for particular problem types.

The following sections include detailed description of the categories of modeling along with narratives of the commonly used solution strategies that have been observed for the Direct Modeling and Counting categories.

Direct Modeling: Direct Modeling is the most concrete category of solution strategies. Direct Modeling is a directly observable task where the child manipulates physical tools including fingers or blocks to organize and represent the problem's components. Direct Modeling can include physically producing objects such as shapes or tally marks on a piece of paper. These physical objects are used to manage all of the information and quantities for solving the word problem. For the addition and subtraction word problems, six common Direct Modeling solution strategies have been observed and categorized. Those six strategies are (a) Joining All, (b) Joining To, (c) Separating From, (d) Separating To, (e) Matching and (f) Trial and Error.

Joining To Strategy: Joining To is a solution strategy where the child begins with a group of objects based upon of the smaller number presented in the problem. Then, s/he uses more objects to join to the smaller number until it totals the larger number that was presented in the problem. Finally, the child counts the group that was added to the smaller group to find the correct answer. The Joining To solution strategy is used to solve Join, Change Unknown problems.

Separating From Strategy: Separating From is a solution strategy that begins with the child representing the larger number presented in the problem. Then, the smaller number is separated from the larger group. The remaining objects are counted to find the correct answer to the problem. The Separating From solution strategy is used to solve Separate, Results Unknown problems.

Separating To Strategy: Separating To is a direct modeling solution strategy where the child starts by using objects to represent the larger number presented in the problem. Then, objects are removed from the larger group until the original set equals the smaller number presented in the problem. In other words, the child separates the smaller number from the larger number. Finally, the child counts how many objects were removed to find the correct answer. The Separating To solution strategy is used for Separate, Change Unknown problems.

Matching Strategy: Matching is a solution strategy used to make one-to-one correspondence between two sets of numbers. First, the child creates two sets of objects, each set representing a respective number as presented in the problem. Then, the child matches pairs between the two groups. Finally, the child counts the remaining unmatched objects from the larger group to find the answer of how many more objects are in the one group. The Matching solution strategy is used for Compare, Difference Unknown problems.

Trial and Error Strategy: Trial and Error is a solution strategy that happens when a child attempts to systematically guess and check possible solutions for the problem until the appropriate relationship is found. To begin, the child will use objects to try different scenarios, while possibly making errors, to discover the correct answer. The Trial-and-Error solution strategy is used for Join, Start Unknown and Separate, Start Unknown problems

For the three multiplication and division problem types, three common Direct Modeling solution strategies have been observed and categorized. Each problem type has its own common solution strategy. The three strategies are (a) Grouping, (b) Measurement and (c) Partitive.

Grouping Strategy: Grouping is a solution strategy where the child uses objects to model each group presented in the problem with the respective number of items in each group. Then, the child will simply count the total of the objects to find the correct answer. The Grouping solution strategy is used for Multiplication problems.

Measurement Strategy: Measurement is a solution strategy that occurs when the number of groups is unknown to the child in the problem. In other words, the child obtains the number of items per group and the total number of items from the word problem. With the known information, the child uses objects to make groups that contain the number of items per group based upon the total number of items. A slight variation of this solution strategy involves whether the child counts the objects for the total number of items at the beginning or ending of the solution process. The child will count the number of groups to find the correct answer. The Measurement solution strategy is used for Measurement Division problems.

Partitive Strategy: Partitive is a solution strategy commonly used when the total number of items and the number of groups are presented in the problem to obtain the solution. Some children may sort the objects one-by-one into the specified number of groups until the objects are used up. Other children may start with more than one object in each group. If the child starts with too few objects per group, he will sort out the remaining objects until no objects remain. If the child begins with too many objects per group, he will remove objects from the groups that were created until the correct number relationship or action is obtained. Finally, the child will count the objects in one group to find the correct answer. The Partitive solution strategy is used for Partitive Division problems.

Counting: Once Direct Modeling concepts become more grounded and instilled during the child's development, Counting solution strategies become more frequent. Counting strategies are more abstract because the child moves from using physical objects to mental representations of numbers in the word problems. Otherwise, the idea of organizing the information and modeling of objects is still rather similar for Counting as it was for Direct Modeling. A child may use physical tools while using a Counting strategy, but the tool is only used for organization, such as to keep track of a number count. For a Counting strategy, the mental representations of the child's mathematical understanding must occur while an organizational tool is used.

Distinct counting strategies commonly used by children have also been observed. Five common counting strategies for addition and subtraction word problems have been categorized. They consist of (a) Counting On, (b) Counting On To, (c) Counting Down, (d) Counting Down To and (e) Trial and Error.

Counting On Strategy: Counting On is a solution strategy where the child mentally counts on from one number with the other number presented in the problem. There are two slightly different variations of Counting On, which are Counting On From First and Counting On From Larger. Counting On From First occurs when the child simply counts on from the first number presented in the problem with the second number. Counting On from Larger happens when the child begins counting from the larger number presented in the problem by the smaller number. For both variations of the Counting On strategy, the final correct answer is the total of both numbers that were presented in the problem. This solution strategy is used for Join, Result Unknown and Part, Part, Whole, Whole Unknown problems.

All problems can be solved by many children who are as young as kindergartners or first graders, if they are given opportunity to model the problem situations. These strategies provide a foundation for the development of more abstract ways of solving problems and thinking about numbers that involve counting. CGI goes on to address algebra and geometry, fractions and decimals (Empson & Levi, 2011).

Examples of CGI Activities

Basic Join Problem Type Examples
Join, Result Unknown: Terry has 3 marbles (Start). Mark gives him 5 more marbles (Change). How many marbles does Terry have altogether (Result Unknown)?

Join, Change Unknown: Terry has 3 marbles (Start). Mark gives him some more marbles. Then Terry has 8 marbles altogether (Result). How many marbles did Mark give to Terry (Change Unknown)?

Join, Start Unknown: Terry has some marbles. Mark gives him 5 more marbles (Change). Then Terry has 8 marbles in total (Result). How many marbles did Terry have to start with (Start Unknown)?

Basic Separate Problem Type Examples
Separate, Result Unknown: Jacinta has 7 marbles (Start). She gives 4 marbles to Lesley (Change). How many marbles does Jacinta have left (Result Unknown)?

Separate, Change Unknown: Jacinta has 7 marbles (Start). She gives some marbles to Lesley. Then Jacinta has 3 marbles left (Result). How many marbles did Jacinta give to Lesley (Change Unknown)?

Separate, Start Unknown Jacinta has some marbles. She gives Lesley 4 marbles (Change). Then Jacinta has 3 marbles left (Result). How many marbles did Jacinta begin with (Start Unknown)?

Basic Part-Part-Whole Problem Type Examples
Part-Part-Whole, Whole Unknown: Jill has 2 blue marbles (Part) and 3 red marbles (Part). How many marbles does she have in total (Whole Unknown)?

Part-Part-Whole, Part Unknown: Jill has 5 marbles (Whole). There are 2 blue marbles (Part) and the rest of the marbles are red. How many of the marbles are red marbles (Part Unknown)?

Basic Compare Problem Type Examples

Compare, Difference Unknown: Pedro has 6 marbles (Referent). Manolo has 10 marbles (Compare Quantity). How many more marbles does Manolo have than Pedro (Difference Unknown)?

Compare, Compare Quantity Unknown: Pedro has 6 marbles (Referent). Manolo has 4 more marbles than Pedro (Difference). How many marbles does Manolo have (Compare Quantity Unknown)?

Compare, Referent Unknown: Pedro has 10 marbles (Compare Quantity). He has 4 more marbles than Manolo. (Difference) How many marbles does Manolo have (Referent Unknown)?

Basic Multiplication and Division Problem Type Examples

Multiplication: Juan has 4 bags of marbles (Number of Groups). There are 5 marbles in each bag (Number of Items per Group). How many marbles does Juan have in all (Total Number of Items Unknown)?

Measurement Division: Juan has 20 marbles (Total Number of Items). He also has some bags. He puts 5 marbles into each bag (Number of Items per Group). How many bags does Juan fill (Number of Groups Unknown)?

Partitive Division: Juan has 20 marbles (Total Number of Items). He puts the marbles into 4 bags with the same number of marbles in each bag (Number of Groups). How many marbles are in each bag (Number of Items per Group Unknown)?

Direct Modeling Strategy Examples for Addition and Subtraction

Joining All: Amelie figures out from the problem that 4 and 6 should be combined. First, she makes a group of 4 blocks and a group of 6 blocks. Then, Amelie joins all of the items from both groups and counts a total of 10 blocks for her answer.

Joining To: Amelie understands that she needs to figure out how much it takes to go from 3 to 8. She begins by drawing a group of 3 circles on a sheet of paper. She then joins to that group by drawing more circles until there are 8 total circles. Amelie counts up the additional circles to discover 5 circles for the answer.

Separating From: Amelie believes that she needs to take 4 away from 7 to find her answer. To start, she counts 7 of her fingers to represent the problem. Next, she separates 4 fingers from the original group of 7. She counts up the remaining fingers to find out that 3 fingers is the correct answer.

Separating To: Amelie needs to find the change to the problem that starts at 8 and ends at 6. First, she creates a group of 8 with crayons. Then, she separates down to 6 crayons. Finally, Amelie counts up the objects that she removed and has 2 crayons as her answer.

Matching: Amelie has to figure out how much more 9 is than 5. She starts by making a group of 9 shapes on her paper. She then makes a group of 5 shapes on her paper. Next, she matches pairs of shapes between the groups, one-by-one, until there are no more available pairs. Finally, she counts up the unmatched shapes and has 4 shapes for the solution.

Trial and Error: Amelie is given a problem where there is a loss of 7 and a final point of 6. First, she tries to begin with a group of 11 blocks. Then, she takes 7 pencils away from the original group and learns that leaves her with 4 pencils, which is an error and falls short of the correct answer. Next, Amelie attempts the process again with a larger starting group, a group of 13 pencils. She takes 7 objects away and has 6 pencils remaining, which is the answer she is supposed to have. Amelie discovers that 13 pencils is the correct answer to the problem.

Direct Modeling Strategy Examples for Multiplication and Division
Grouping: José has a problem where there are 4 groups with 5 objects in each group. He starts by making one group with 5 blocks. José repeats that step until he has 4 groups with 5 blocks in each group. Finally, he counts up all of the blocks to discover that 20 blocks is the answer.

Measurement: José needs to figure out how many groups come from having 18 total pencils and 3 pencils in each group. First, he counts out 18 pencils. Then, he makes one group with

3 pencils. José continues the same process until all of the pencils are in a group. Finally, he counts up all of the groups that he made and has 6 groups as the answer.

Partitive: José encounters a problem that explains there are 12 total objects and 3 groups with the same number of items in each group. With that information, he works to find how many items are in each group. José begins by constructing a group of 12 cubes. Next, he puts the cubes one-by-one into 3 different groups. Once he divides all of the cubes into equally sized groups, José counts 4 cubes in each group for the answer.

Counting Strategy Examples for Addition and Subtraction

Counting On: Luis receives a problem where he must add 9 and 4. He starts at the number 9 and orally counts on 4 more units. When he finishes at the last number, Luis realizes that the answer is 13.

Counting On To: Luis must figure out how much it takes to go from 7 to 15. He begins at 7 and mentally counts on until he gets up to 15. He keeps track of the amount between the two numbers and determines that 8 is his answer.

Counting Down: Luis has to subtract 6 from 11. First, he begins at 11 and silently counts down 6 units. Luis discovers that the amount he is left with is 5, which is the correct answer.

Counting Down To: Luis encounters a problem where he must find the amount it takes to go from 17 to 8. He starts at 17 and counts down to 8 aloud. While he is counting backward, Luis pays attention to the amount between 17 and 8. He finds out that the solution is 9.

Trial and Error: Luis must find the starting point to a problem containing a gain of 5 and a final amount of 14. First, he tries beginning at 8. Next, he counts on 5 more units to 8 to get 13, which he realizes is an error. Luis attempts the process over again instead he begins with 9. After adding 5 to nine and getting 14, he learns that 9 is the correct answer.

Counting Strategy Examples for Multiplication and Division

Skip-Counting: Valeria has a problem where there are 6 groups and 5 items in each group. Since she knows how to count by 5s, she begins counting aloud 5, 10, 15, 20, 25 and finally 30. She learns that 6 groups of 5 items equals 30, which is the correct answer.

Addition and Subtraction Strategies: Valeria works to figure out a question that has 8 groups with 3 items in each group. First, she writes down the number 3 eight times. Second, she starts to double up pairs of numbers into groups. From the 8 groups of 3, Valeria gets 4 groups of 6. Next, from the 4 groups of 6, she makes 2 groups of 12. Finally, she puts the 2 groups of 12 together to have 24 as her answer.

Trial and Error: Valeria attempts to solve a problem where the number of items is unknown. She knows that there are 3 groups with the same number in each group and that there are 27 total items. First, Valeria starts by counting 3 groups with 7 items per group, and she realizes that there are too few total items from this situation. Next, she tries counting 3 groups with 11 items per group and determines that there are too many total items this time. Then, Valeria attempts to count 3 groups with 9 items in each group. With 9 items in each group, she finds the solution for the problem.

Training for CGI

The CGI professional development program consists of a series of activities that provide the analyses of types of mathematical problems, children's informal strategies for different kinds of problems and a developmental trajectory of children's understanding of arithmetic.

Children learn certain number combinations in and out of school without specific drills for memorizing number facts. They often use a small number of memorized facts to derive solutions for other problems with other numbers – these are known as derived facts. In professional development programs, teachers discuss how to use various problem types to facilitate children to make sense of situations and construct their own strategies. Professional development provides teachers with structured knowledge of the semantic differences of problems and underlying conceptual issues in the areas of place value, multi-digit addition and subtraction, multiplication and division and geometry. CGI has been recognized as applicable for students of all ability levels and those with special needs and language barrier issues.

The initial CGI workshops involved meeting once a week. The five themes emphasized were: (1) children who are exposed to a variety of problems can learn important mathematical ideas, (2) individuals and groups of children will come up with a variety of solutions to the same problem, (3) talking and writing about mathematics is important for student learning, (4) teachers need to know what students are thinking and (5) what students currently know and understand should affect the way instruction is delivered in the classroom. Videotapes of students solving problems and classroom discussion were the two main strategies used in the workshop to convey these five ideas to teachers.

As the participants viewed video clips of students as they solved problems, they were told to focus on the thinking of students. After the clip, the participants talked about what they saw. The types of items discussed might be: (a) how the student saw the problem, (b) what approach the student took in solving the problem and what that meant in terms of the child's conceptual abilities, (c) why the solution worked and how it was different from other solutions, (d) how might this student solve other types of problems, and (d) how this student's solution might indicate the student's overall understanding of different concepts.

Teachers were encouraged to attempt the same problems seen on the video with their own students during the week. Some teachers did this and reported their experiences to the rest of the group the following week. These workshops were participant led. After the workshops were concluded, the program staff followed the participants into their schools. A CGI staff member and a mentor teacher were assigned to each school that had a participant in the workshop. These two persons had the responsibility of meeting with the participants throughout the school year (on more or less a weekly basis). Their main role, in the same spirit as the workshops, was to provide participants an opportunity to discuss what was happening in their classroom in terms of student thinking and instructional choices.

Teacher education materials have been developed for both in-service and pre-service teachers. These materials include chapters detailing CGI philosophy; the content analyses of addition/subtraction, multiplication/division, place value and multidigit algorithms, functions and geometry; children's thinking; and videotapes that illustrate children's thinking and prototypic classrooms. Carpenter and colleagues produced a CGI book with a supplementary CD of videos for teachers (Carpenter et al., 1999) and a book for workshop leaders (Fennema et al., 1999). In addition to these is a further book on fractions and decimals by Empson and Levi (2011).

There have been several studies of the effectiveness of the PD program. For example, Moscardini (2014) introduced CGI to 21 mainstream elementary teachers. The findings demonstrate how increased understanding of children's mathematical thinking left the teachers better placed to support all learners. In 2018, Conowal studied ten elementary mathematics teachers, using interviews and classroom observations. Findings identified positive results from CGI techniques, with students showing learning levels beyond their grades and developing creative problem-solving techniques that were beneficial for the current curriculum and for future grade levels as well. The most significant deterrent for CGI use was the time investment required to carry out the lessons or exercises in ways that incorporated CGI practices.

Gadge (2018) investigated the effects of a two-year-long CGI PD on teachers' instructional practices in elementary classrooms. Forty-two and 47 classrooms were observed and videotaped during the first and second years, respectively. CGI PD involved four days in each of the two summers and two sets of two-day follow-up sessions during the school year in each of the two years when the study was conducted. Classroom instruction was videotaped and the resulting data were analyzed using logistic regression. CGI teachers were more likely than non-CGI teachers to provide their students with various problem-solving opportunities by implementing instructional processes such as: posing high-cognitive tasks; posing word problems; implementing tasks at high-cognitive levels; spending time on single problems; allowing students to choose their solution method; providing access to manipulatives; encouraging multiple strategies; giving students time to solve problems; asking students to share their solutions; spending time discussing problem as a whole class; and listening to student thinking of solutions (all of these were significantly different between groups in both first- and second-grade classrooms, across two years of investigation). On average, CGI teachers were ten times more likely to do something as compared to non-CGI control teachers. This suggests CGI PD had a large positive effect on teacher instruction of problem-solving.

Extensions of CGI

As we have noted, CGI now extends across many areas of mathematics, including fractions and algebra and geometry. It has been used in many countries, including countries not having English as a first language.

References and Bibliography

Carpenter, T. P., Ansell, E., Franke, M. L., Fennema, E., & Weisbeck, L. (1993). Models of problem solving: A study of kindergarten children's problem-solving processes. *Journal for Research in Mathematics Education*, *24*(5), 428–441. https://doi.org/10.5951/jresematheduc.24.5.0428

Carpenter, T. P., Fennema, E., Franke, M. L., Levi, L., & Empson, S. B. (1999). *Children's mathematics: Cognitively Guided Instruction*. Portsmouth, NH: Heinemann.

Carpenter, T. P., Fennema, E., Franke, M. L., Levi, L., & Empson, S. B. (2015). *Children's mathematics: Cognitively Guided Instruction* (second edition). Portsmouth, NH: Heinemann.

Carpenter. T. P., Fennema, E., Peterson. P. L., Chiang, C. P., & Lod, M. (1989). Using knowledge of children's mathematics thinking in classroom teaching: An experimental study. *American Educational Research Journal*, *26*(4), 499–531.

Conowal, T. A. (2018). *Cognitively Guided Instruction in elementary mathematics: Understanding factors that influence classroom implementation*. Doctor of Education dissertation, Kennesaw State University. https://digitalcommons.kennesaw.edu/teachleaddoc_etd/25

Empson, S. B., & Levi, L. (2011). *Extending children's mathematics: Fractions and decimals*. Portsmouth, NH: Heinemann.

Fennema, E., Carpenter, T. P., Franke, M. L., Levi, L., & Empson, S. B. (1999). *Children's mathematics: Cognitively Guided Instruction - A guide for workshop leaders*. Portsmouth, NH: Heinemann.

Gadge, U. (2018). *Effects of Cognitively Guided Instruction on teacher created opportunities to engage students in problem-solving*. Doctoral dissertation, University of Miami. https://scholarship.miami.edu/discovery/fulldisplay/alma991031447698402976/01UOML_INST:ResearchRepository

Moscardini, L. (2014). Developing equitable elementary mathematics classrooms through teachers learning about children's mathematical thinking: Cognitively Guided Instruction as an inclusive pedagogy. *Teaching and Teacher Education*, *43*, 69–79. https://doi.org/10.1016/j.tate.2014.06.003

Schoen, R. C., LaVenia, M., & Tazaz, A. M. (2018). *Effects of the first year of a three-year CGI teacher professional development program on grades 3–5 student achievement: A multisite cluster-randomized trial* (Research Report No. 2018-25). Tallahassee, FL: Learning Systems Institute, Florida State University. http://doi.org/10.33009/fsu.1562595733

Schoen, R. C., Rhoads, C., Perez, A. L., Tazaz, A. M., & Secada, W. G. (2022). *Impact of Cognitively Guided Instruction on elementary school mathematics achievement: Five years after the initial opportunity*. Tallahassee, FL: Florida State University. https://doi.org/10.33009/fsu.1653430141

Villasenor, A., & Kepner, H. S. (1993). Arithmetic from a problem–solving perspective: An urban implementation. *Journal for Research in Mathematics*, *24*(1), 62–69. https://doi.org/10.5951/jresematheduc.24.1.0062

4

Reading

Paired Reading and Thinking

Paired *Reading* (PR) is a reading peer tutoring method for cross-ability pairs. Working with self-chosen books above the independent readability level of the tutee, the tutor reads together on difficult parts but encourages independent reading on easier parts. There is a simple correction procedure. Paired *Thinking* (PT) goes beyond this by developing dialogue about the book, with the tutor asking questions to ensure understanding of the text. This questioning is initially scaffolded by four levels of prompt questions of increasing difficulty. Although much reading comprehension is based on reading fiction, of course it is also relevant to reading non-fiction (although the scaffolding questions may need revising to reflect this change of context), which of course could be in any subject area. Thus, Paired Thinking could apply to any subject. Of course, Paired Thinking could be used with any other reading tutoring method.

Paired Thinking was originated by Keith Topping. It is extensively described in his book: *Thinking, Reading, Writing: A Practical Guide to Paired Learning with Peers, Parents and Volunteers* (with accompanying website of free resources https://sites.dundee.ac.uk/keith-topping/thinking-reading-writing). A video is also available at cost – contact Keith Topping at k.j.topping@dundee.ac.uk.

Effects of Paired Thinking

The Paired Reading method has now been very widely disseminated all over the world and has been demonstrated to be effective with thousands of children in hundreds of schools. It has been the subject of many research reviews. There are many controlled studies demonstrating effectiveness. Follow-up studies indicate that gains are sustained and do not wash out over time. Paired Thinking is typically deployed as an extension to PR, participants first receiving training in and experiencing practice of PR, before receiving further training in PT.

Topping and Bryce (2004) described and evaluated a method for PT, which scaffolded interactive discourse based on a differentiated real book the tutorial pair had chosen to read together. This study aimed to partial the impact on quality of thinking of a peer-tutored thinking intervention from that of a peer-tutored reading intervention, controlling for time on task and amount of peer interactivity. Experimental peer tutees were a whole class ($n = 28$) of 7-year-olds; experimental tutors a whole class ($n = 31$) of 11-year-olds. Comparison tutees were a whole class ($n = 27$) of 7-year-olds; comparison tutors a whole class ($n = 30$) of 11-year-olds. Classes/teachers within the same school were randomly assigned to conditions.

In Phase 1, a paired reading intervention was implemented for six weeks for all groups. In Phase 2, the experimental classes of tutors and tutees engaged in the "Paired Thinking" (PT) method for ten weeks, while the comparison group continued with paired reading. Both treatments involved one 20-minute session weekly. Pre- and post-test assessment of thinking skills and attitude to reading for all participants was conducted and post hoc subjective feedback gathered from participants. The experimental (PT) tutees showed significantly better performance in thinking skills than comparison (PR only) tutees and some evidence of improved attitudes to reading. However, this was not true for the experimental (PT) tutors. Subjective feedback was very positive from the PT tutees and class teachers, but less positive from the PT tutors, who found the process hard work.

Given the brevity and low cost in time and resources of the treatment, the finding of significant differences in measured thinking skills for the PT tutees is considered encouraging. The lack of evidence of progress for the PT tutors was surprising, since the tutors often gain more than the tutees.

The Paired Thinking method was then tried in a high school by McKinstery and Topping (2003). Paired Reading operated for four weeks, then further training meetings preceded the move to Paired Thinking, which operated for a further five weeks. Pre-post assessment of reading comprehension for tutees and perceptions of tutors and teachers spanned both PR and PT phases. Subjective feedback from tutees, tutors and teachers was gathered by post hoc questionnaire and interview. It was not possible to establish control groups. However, the relatively high levels of ability, maturity and insight in the tutor group meant that their own reflective observations on their experiences were likely to be a rich source of information. The project was interesting organizationally as it was led, coordinated and monitored internally by the head of mathematics, although the English department was also involved.

The tutors were volunteers from the fifth and sixth years (16–18 years old). Eighteen initially volunteered (12 females and six males). Tutees were randomly chosen from one mixed ability class group in first year (12-year-olds). Owing to an imbalance of gender in the tutee class, nine tutees were female and six were male. The resulting constellations were six cross-gender pairings and nine same-gender pairings. There was free student selection of reading materials from any source, including the school library and English department resources — both fiction and non-fiction. The four levels of PT prompt sheet were color-coded to allow the monitoring adults to see at a glance the level at which any pair was working.

Training meetings were held first for the tutors only, then for the tutors and tutees together. PR training for all groups involved verbal instruction, demonstration, a written reminder, practice, coaching and feedback. At the second training meeting participants were issued personal copies of the Level 1 prompt sheet. A researcher explained the techniques involved using the reading exemplar and prompt sheet, emphasizing the type of questions that could be utilized before, during and after reading. The different levels of questioning were explained. A researcher then modeled questioning on a whole-class basis using the reading exemplar, emphasizing active listening and thinking aloud. Practice followed in the established pairings, while a researcher and class teachers monitored and gave further coaching as needed. Tutors were issued with the Tips for Tutors sheet (see below).

PR and PT sessions took place three times per week, each session lasting approximately 20 minutes. Due to the differing timetables of the tutors, session days and times were idiosyncratic to each pair. This involved tutees being released from several subject classes throughout the week and required synchronization from the coordinating teacher. The tutors and tutees were largely responsible for ensuring their own meetings took place. The school library and the senior social area were made available for the sessions. A researcher monitored the sessions on a twice-weekly basis. A monitoring checklist was utilized on these occasions. Interim meetings were also held with the tutors to review and check technique.

On Reading Comprehension, at pre-test the mean reading age was 13 years 2 months, at post-test it was 14 years 0 months — an increase of 10 months in reading age over a four-month period. This gain is much greater than would be expected, and was statistically significant ($p = 0.05$). Tutee statements concerning what they liked about PT included: the discussions were enjoyable (more than one-half of the tutees said this); the tutor was friendly; the tutor explained the book/words; getting out of regular classes; and PT was hard (*sic*). When asked what they disliked about PT: 33% stated that they disliked the questioning as they found it difficult; 3% found the tutee/tutor relationship problematic and 20% found that meeting their tutor at a specific time could be difficult. However, when asked if they found it easy to answer questions during the session, 70% of tutees answered in the affirmative. Tutors were asked about progression in or transference of thinking skills.

Ninety per cent thought that their own thinking skills and those of their tutee had improved.

Supporting statements included: the tutee became more adept at reasoning; discussing things that the tutee did not understand helped me to elaborate on my thinking; and I had to respond to the tutee's questions, which helped me to analyze more.

Theoretical Underpinnings of Paired Thinking

The theoretical underpinnings of Paired Reading have been explained in Topping and Lindsay (1992). The development into Paired Thinking was based on behavioral psychology, then extended into pragmatics rather than theory, but echoes the work of Mercer et al. (2020) on dialogic reading, while giving more structure to the discussion. PT features a gradual progression into more complex thinking to be accessible to students of all ages and abilities.

Structure and Implementation of Paired Thinking (PT)

The PT program and materials embed the teaching of thinking skills in the transferable skill of reading. PT is a framework for pairs working together. Some difference in reading ability is needed in each pair. The pairs can be peers of the same or different ages, parents working with children at home, teaching assistants working with children in school or volunteer adults (such as senior citizens) working with children in school.

The PT method provides:

- Modeling of intelligent questioning for the tutee
- Interactive cognitive challenge for both partners
- Practice in critical and analytic thinking
- Scaffolding
- Feedback
- Praise and other social reinforcement

PT also:

- Flexibly applies to any reading experience chosen and shared by the pair
- Enables the pair to pursue their own interests and motivations
- Is highly adaptable to the individual learner's needs of the moment
- Is democratic and encourages learner-managed learning
- Encourages critical and analytic discussion in the pair's vernacular vocabulary
- Encourages self-disclosure of faulty or deficient thinking.

The PT structure of 13 activities within three stages is outlined in Table 4.1, with an example (model or prompt) question for each activity. The 13 activities are supported by prompt sheets of questions, available in four differentiated levels of complexity and difficulty, to suit different pairs and provide developmental progression. However, tutors are strongly encouraged to view the prompt sheet only as a training and fallback resource, and to generate their own questions of high relevance to the text and their partner.

The 13 example questions listed constitute the whole content of the Level 1 question prompt sheet. For training, all pairs start with a Level 1 prompt sheet. As pairs progress at different rates in subsequent sessions, Level 2, Level 3 and Level 4 prompt sheets (each adding more questions and more complex questions) can be issued to particular pairs as the teacher considers optimal, progressively differentiating and individualizing the activity (see Appendix 1).

As an example of this progression, readers might wish to compare the prompt questions at each level for one activity (Prediction). In this activity, Level 1 prompts with a single question: What might happen next? Level 2 offers five questions, including: What might make this happen? How likely is this? Level 3 offers 10 questions, including: What do the people in the book want or expect to happen next? What have you learned about them that helps you to guess what they might do next?

TABLE 4.1
Stages, Activities and Levels in Paired Thinking

Paired Thinking
(Read – Think – Feel – Talk – Listen)
Asking each other intelligent questions about what we have read together
3 Stages (Before, During, After Reading)
13 Activities
4 Levels
21 Sub-categories
21 Tips for Tutors
Lots of Questions (Prompts)

BEFORE READING
(Priming)

Structure	"What do the parts of the book tell us?"
Type	"What kind of book is it?"
Difficulty	"How hard is it?
Reader Aims	"What do you want from the book?"

DURING READING
(Formative)

Author Aims	"What does the writer want?"
Meaning	"What does it mean?"
Truth	"Is it true?"
Prediction	"What might happen next?"
Links	"What does it remind us of?"

AFTER READING
(Formative & Summative)

Summarize	"What are the main ideas?"
Evaluate	"How do you feel about it?"
Revisit	"What did you remember about it?"
Extend	"Have you questioned anything else?"

Level 4 offers 16 questions, including: What might cause this to happen? How would you know what had really caused it? Will it only happen if something else happens?

The levels enable young and less able readers to participate but provide extension for higher ability and age ranges. Level 4 is perhaps better suited to high school or even college students. At all levels, the intellectual strain on the tutor is quite considerable. Indeed, as in other applications of peer tutoring, there is now more interest among both researchers and practitioners in the impact of being a tutor than on the value of being a tutee.

The interactive behavior required is outlined in a Tips for Tutors handout (see below). These are abbreviated for everyday use in a Tips for Tutors Reminder sheet. When initially presenting them to pairs in training, teachers often present just a few at a time and not necessarily in this order.

Paired Thinking – Tips for Tutors

Your **aim** is to **improve** the tutee's **quality of thinking** by asking helpful and **intelligent questions** which give clues. This is not as easy as you might think! Tutors have to think hard, too – they do not just work through a list of given questions.

You need to put tutees at their ease, boost their confidence, and **encourage** them to trust you – or they will be afraid to let you know what they are thinking.

During reading, pause quite often at any **natural break** in the reading to think and talk about what you have read.

Remember tutees are not as old as you and don't know as much as you do, so **don't expect too much** or push them too hard.

Encourage tutees to **"think aloud"**, so you can hear *how* they are thinking and really understand them – if they think alone then just give you their final answer, you will not understand how they got there. You might "think aloud" yourself sometimes, to show them how to do it.

Sometimes you can also try to **"brainstorm"** answers – this is where both of you say every possible answer that comes into your head, even if it seems silly or weird. Then choose the best.

Never say "No" or "That's wrong" – always ask another question to give a clue.

Although there are many questions, **it is not a "test"** for the tutee. Indeed, often **there is no one "right" answer**, only many "better" or "worse" answers. Work toward getting more "better" answers. But even the tutor need not know the answer to the question at the beginning – you can work it out together.

Tutees can ask tutors **questions**, too! Keep each other thinking!

It's OK for both tutors and tutees **to say** they **"don't know"** – but be clear about what you need to know and think about how you might find out.

Give the tutees some **time to think** – they will not usually be able to answer straightaway. But if they think for more than half a minute without success, maybe they need a clue in another question.

Praise the tutee for all thoughtful responses – for example: "Good, I can tell you thought hard about that".

The questions listed are only examples to get you started - please do **think up your own questions** as well. Your own questions should encourage the tutee to say whatever they really think, not push them toward one "right answer".

Tutors can say what they think, too – but be careful not let tutees assume that must be the "right answer" – ask the tutee what they think as well.

You might need to go back to **read bits** of the book **again** at any time to check on things or answer questions. When you do, you might want to read the difficult bit *to* the tutee, so they can think about it.

Some of the listed questions apply only to story books, some apply only to information books. Just **leave out the questions which don't apply** to the book you are reading.

When you are stuck trying to think of a question quickly, **"How do you know that?"** is often a good one.

When you are reading a longer book, you might find the tutee has trouble **remembering** everything, even if they did understand it in the first place. If they don't remember, it does not always mean they never did **understand**.

You might find tutees remember the beginning or end of a book better than the middle – but they do need to think about the middle as well!

In the "BEFORE" Stage, the **"Five Finger Test"** for difficulty of book means you:

- spread out 5 fingers on one hand
- choose any page of the book
- put the 5 fingers down on the text
- see if you can read all 5 words correctly
- repeat on another 3 pages.

If the tutor struggles to read more than one or two of the 20 "fingered" words, the book is probably too hard for the tutor.

In the "DURING READING" Stage, the five Activities (Author Aims, Meaning, Truth, Prediction, Links) can be worked through in **any order**. Choose any relevant questions from any Activity at any time.

In the "AFTER READING" Stage when you are finding the main ideas or "Summarizing" and choose to write down some keywords and/or write a summary for your classmates, it is usually **easier** if the **tutor does any writing** – but the tutor must not do all the thinking!

In the "AFTER READING" Stage when you are doing "Self-Assessment", this is a good time to really **praise** each other – AGAIN!

The four prompt sheets will be found in Appendix 1.

Examples of Paired Thinking Activities

As all Paired Reading and Paired Thinking activities are determined by the tutorial pair, based on a book they have individually chosen, it is impossible to give example activities without going into great length.

Training for Paired Thinking

Training for Paired Reading is typically done in one meeting of about one-and-a-half hours, which involves both tutors and tutees (be they peers, parents and students or volunteer tutors and students). Participants are given verbal instruction about the method, written information to take away as a reminder and a demonstration of how to do it (often on video but can be live between members of staff role playing or between a teacher and a student if you have a student who has robust performance skills). Pairs then take books made available and practice the method, while project staff circulate to monitor and coach. A fixed time of commitment is set, after which participants will consider whether they wish to continue or not. Training for Paired Thinking is very similar. The pairs will already be familiar with Paired Reading, so it is merely a question of extending their understanding into more complex questioning and thinking.

Of course, this omits the question of what happens during the subsequent tutoring sessions themselves and the teacher should certainly be monitoring where these are in class and coaching to keep implementation integrity as high as possible. After the initial period of commitment, a review meeting should be held where pairs discuss options and decide what they want to do.

Extensions of Paired Thinking

We have already noted that Paired Thinking can be operated with any reading tutoring program and this gives a wide range of options. Additionally, we have also noted that Paired Thinking can be done with both fiction and non-fiction books. Although the Prompt Sheets are designed to be used with fiction books, it would be perfectly possible to design another set to be used with non-fiction books. This would then enable Paired Thinking to operate in any subject area of the curriculum, using textbooks or research project books available within the school.

References and Bibliography

McKinstery, J., & Topping, K. J. (2003). Cross-age peer tutoring of thinking skills in the high school. *Educational Psychology in Practice, 19*(3), 199–217. https://doi.org/10.1080/0266736032000109465

Mercer, N., Wegerif, R., & Major, L. (2020). *The Routledge international handbook of research on dialogic education*. London & New York: Routledge.

Topping, K. J. (2001). *Thinking reading writing: A practical guide to paired Learning with peers, parents and volunteers*. London & New York: Continuum. Resource website: https://sites.dundee.ac.uk/keith-topping/thinking-reading-writing

Topping, K. J., & Bryce, A. (2004). Cross-age peer tutoring of reading and thinking: Influence on thinking skills. *Educational Psychology: An International Journal of Experimental Educational Psychology, 24*(5), 595–621. http://dx.doi.org/10.1080/0144341042000262935

Topping, K. J., & Lindsay, G. A. (1992). The structure and development of the Paired Reading technique. *The Journal of Research in Reading, 15*(2), 120–136. https://doi.org/10.1111/j.1467-9817.1992.tb00028.x

5

Geography

Thinking Through Geography (TTG)

Geography is a separate subject in the UK but usually incorporated in social studies in the USA. However, the methods described here can be applied to any curriculum subject. Teachers become interested in developing *critical thinking in practice*, identifying three aspects to this in Geography: (1) *Becoming better at thinking*, for example through developing students'/pupils' ability to ask good questions and reflect on their learning. Here critical thinking helped strengthen curiosity and the first stages of investigations; (2) *Making better sense of information, knowledge and ideas*, such as by examining evidence, learning to distinguish fact from opinion and considering alternative solutions to problems. Here critical thinking helped build informed understanding; and (3) *Becoming a more open thinker*, such as by challenging assumptions through critical thinking, which helped students/pupils evaluate and become more autonomous learners, able to think through and reach their own well-founded opinions, based on evidence – which may also have helped make them more resilient to others' opinions. Teachers found students began to ask more questions and realized that debriefing following the activity was the most important part for transfer of learning.

Thinking Through Geography was developed by a team of teachers working with David Leat at Newcastle University in the UK. This resulted in books such as Leat (2001), Nichols and Kinninment (2001), Nichols, Kinninment and Leat (2005) and a chapter: Leat (2002). The ideas of Thinking Through Geography then spread to the Netherlands (where Joop van der Schee and Leon Vankan were very active) and on to Germany. In recent years other researchers have discussed the notion of conceptual development through geography (e.g., Cox et al. 2020).

These authors noted that systems thinking helps students to understand increasing complexity by looking at the entire system and the interconnectedness between the elements in the system. A measuring tool was developed, taken by 735 students aged 16–18 years in Belgium. Students had a poor general level of systems thinking ability and many difficulties recognizing relationships between variables such as in feedback loops, interactions between the human and physical environment and a combination of different information sources. There was an interaction effect between grade and gender of the students.

Effects of Thinking Through Geography

Most of the evaluation evidence on effects comes from the Netherlands. Van der Schee et al. (2003) reported that workshops lasting two days were organized for 90 geography teachers in the Netherlands. Strategy exemplars published in the Thinking Through Geography books were translated into Dutch. After both days teachers answered a questionnaire. Two-thirds of the teachers did not know anything about the TTG work before, while one-third had some familiarity, but only 5% had used a thinking strategy in their classes. Almost all teachers (96%) responded that the workshops had given them useful ideas for their own teaching practice. Teachers gave a mark between 1 and 10 for the usability of the strategies and the average score was 7.2.

Between three to nine months after similar workshops, Leat et al. (2005) reported feedback from 90 teachers selected at random from 500 geography teachers who followed a TTG training. They responded to a questionnaire investigating whether they really used the strategies in their geography lessons. All teachers, except one, that returned the questionnaire used one or more of the TTG strategies in their class, but the response rate was only 36%. The in-service training started with some simple and short strategies. The more complex and longer strategies were introduced at the end. Teachers preferred to use the simple and short strategies like Taboo and Odd One Out. Quite a lot of teachers adapted the simpler strategies to other content in their geography class, but few adapted the more complex strategies.

The experimental group in a pilot school showed a significant increase in total score between pre-test and post-test, whereas the control group had a significant decrease. The experimental groups at further schools had a significantly higher total score on the post-test than on the pre-test. Surprisingly, the control group of School 3 also showed a significant increase in total score between pre-test and post-test. All control groups followed lessons from their regular geography schoolbook. The roles of the different teachers and different materials in the control groups may explain some of these differences. In addition, the videotapes of the debriefings in the experimental groups show big differences between the teachers in the amount of attention given to thinking skills processes. All participating teachers stressed the importance of the debriefing. Good debriefing encouraged students to make connections between existing and new learning and provided heuristics.

An experiment in three Dutch lower secondary schools was reported by van der Schee et al. (2006). In all schools three Thinking Through Geography strategies were tested in a quasi-experimental pre-test and post-test control group design. All six classes had the same age group (13 or 14 years of age) and the same intellectual level (second year grammar school). The total number of students at the three schools participating was 153, divided into experimental and control. The three strategies used in the experimental group were Dutch adaptations of "Five Ws", "Reading Photographs" and "Mystery". These three strategies were chosen because they challenged students to classify information and relate different facts and concepts. The control group followed lessons from their regular geography schoolbook.

Time allocated was three lessons of 50 minutes, excluding the pre-test and post-test, which were the same. The test consisted of 20 open questions and was based on the "Odd One Out" strategy from the TTG book. More than 50% of the lessons of the experimental groups in the three schools were observed and videotaped. In some of the experimental classes, teachers also interviewed students. All the students worked enthusiastically with the strategies, but there were big differences in the results between the schools. One of the key factors seems to be the role of the teacher.

Hooghuis et al. (2014) noted that research suggested that teachers acquainted with TTG did not always take full advantage of the possibilities of these strategies. A survey of Dutch geography teachers ($n = 340$ from 81 schools) regarding the significance they assigned to geographical reasoning and their use of TTG assignments was reported. The results suggested that teachers used TTG selectively and adapted TTG assignments to fit into existing practices and beliefs about students and teaching geography. The higher the educational level of the students, the more importance was attached to geographical reasoning. Time spent in class on geographical reasoning also showed differences between the educational levels of the students.

A discussion of the relevance of TTG to understanding the effects of the Covid pandemic across countries was offered by van der Schee (2020). This brought TTG very much up to date.

Theoretical Underpinnings of Thinking Through Geography

The theoretical framework used by TTG has very eclectic roots, influenced by CASE (Adey & Shayer, see Chapter 2), Instrumental Enrichment (Feuerstein, see Chapter 9) and Community of Enquiry (Lipman, see Chapter 12). Like other recent efforts for curriculum renewal, TTG theoretically works from a constructivist point of view. However, a report from Applis (2016) in Germany described how teachers worked with methods from the TTG. The results confirmed previous suppositions, that many teachers say that constructivism is the way they have always known people to learn and the same way in which they want to teach, yet many of the same teachers acknowledge that they have not changed their teaching practices accordingly. New information will be understood only if it can be interpreted through existing knowledge structures. An important principle is getting pupils to access their existing knowledge or to provide concrete experiences that will serve as the framework for their understanding of an issue. Furthermore, the role of talk is extremely important, as it allows a broader range of ideas to be explored and students can talk themselves into understanding as they interpret, question, clarify and speculate.

TTG has three broad aims: (1) to devise adaptable strategies and curriculum materials that make geography lessons more stimulating and challenging; (2) to help pupils understand some fundamental concepts and develop some important cognitive skills in geography in an explicit way so that these can be transferred to new contexts; and (3) to aid the intellectual development of pupils so that they can handle more complex information and achieve greater academic success. TTG subscribes to this definition:

> A student can reason geographically, if (s)he can make a plausible statement about the properties and location of a phenomenon, its relationships with other phenomena or areas, its genesis or impact on future developments and, if relevant, can voice an argued opinion on the desirability of the situation or development, through observing, questioning, analyzing and interpreting the landscape, maps, photographs or other sources.

The main assumption of the model is that practice in the classroom is the most significant factor influencing learning outcomes, as the interaction between teacher and pupil is the most significant influence on pupil learning. Interacting with teacher practices are a set of beliefs about what it is to be good at geography, how pupils learn to be good geographers and how best to teach geography. Also influencing practice is the teacher's pedagogical content knowledge, geographical subject knowledge, knowledge of pupils and knowledge of teaching approaches. Furthermore, pupils' responses to changes in teachers' practices can influence whether the changes are reinforced or discouraged. Relationships are not unidirectional and the strength of the relationships may vary. As such, TTG has enormous potential for diagnostic and formative assessment and offers the opportunity of putting into operation Vygotsky's notion of a Zone of Proximal Development.

Geographical knowledge contains an overview of the spatial differentiation on the earth's surface and distinguishing characteristics of places and regions. It involves declarative knowledge (facts, concepts, theories) and procedural knowledge (skills, methods) as in physical and human geography. Geographical reasoning is defined as reasonable reflective thinking about the relationship between humankind and environment focused on deciding what to believe or do in situations where location matters. Critical thinking is, by this definition, an important part of problem solving.

Geographical reasoning presumes a consistent and logical way of thinking leading to conclusions based on explained assumptions and arguments. The conclusion can be an explanation, a prediction, a judgment about the validity of a statement or a statement about the desirability of an action. Reasoning is above all a process of searching for plausibility, which is constrained by time and place and ethically charged. The conclusions are not always unambiguous and the aim has to be to decide which of the possible conclusions is most plausible and acceptable. Key concepts in TTG are the uniqueness, meaning and interdependence of places and regions, the interdependence of geographical scales, the interaction between actors and social structures and the interaction between society and nature.

Structure and Implementation of Thinking Through Geography

Leat and Lin (2003) of the Newcastle TTG group arranged for four experienced teachers to visit each of the other three, and thus also be visited by the other three. There were two priorities in selecting lessons. The first was to select a range of lessons in terms of achievement groupings (low, mixed and high), ages (11–15 years) and experience of debriefing episodes. The debriefing part of the lesson (and in some cases the whole lesson) was videorecorded. Immediately after the lesson, the visiting teacher interviewed a small group of pupils (between three and six) and pursued two broad questions with them. The first was, What did you learn in that lesson? and the second was, What did the teacher do that helped you?

Pedagogically, a complete TTG lesson consists of five stages: (1) introduction, (2) instruction, (3) task execution in small groups, (4) reflective plenary discussion and (5) debriefing. The TTG strategies are classified into eight groups, based on their geographical content and level of complexity: (1) describing and relating concepts, (2) recognizing and using concepts in real-life situations, (3) analyzing and interpretating maps and graphs, (4) analyzing and interpretating photos, movies and stories, (5) analyzing regions, (6) analyzing spatial problems or developments, (7) opinion forming and (8) making and justifying decisions.

TTG strategies have the following characteristics: (1) They provide a structure or template into which teachers can fit the subject content that is their everyday currency. (2) The strategies then make very different demands on pupils in terms of subject knowledge – the knowledge is used by the students to make sense of a challenge or situation. The subject knowledge is used to interpret, reason and speculate. There is much less pressure to get a right answer, but more pressure to make sense and justify. (3) The strategies invite pupils to work together and to use talk to achieve solutions. Cooperative group work is a powerful motivator for most students. (4) The effect of this is to allow teachers to move into a different role in which they are no longer the guardians of right answers but are freed to become mediators of and partners in learning (which does not mean that they never instruct and explain).

The plenary discussion is the crucial element for enabling students to consolidate their learning and the transfer of knowledge to other contexts. It is advised to start the plenary discussion with a presentation of and discussion about possible outcomes.

This should be followed by reflection on argumentation, strategies used or the possibilities for applying knowledge in other domains and contexts. Reserving time for the debriefing stage is very important. For a plenary discussion at least ten minutes are needed.

During debriefing, there were ten roles that teachers often took on:

1. Using stimulating strategies in teaching
2. Attending to groups and individuals
3. Encouraging pupils to ask questions
4. Collating ideas
5. Providing heuristics and alternative representations
6. Promoting and managing discussion
7. Making pupils explain themselves
8. Providing feedback
9. Making connections
10. Communicating the purpose of lessons

TTG has developed a number of curriculum units and identified and clarified a number of principles for curriculum design and teaching. The books each contain eight powerful pedagogical strategies with three exemplars of their use in varied geography teaching contexts. They include background information on the strategies together with the classroom materials used and, based on the classroom trials, advice on planning, introducing the tasks in the classroom, managing the group work, debriefing the learning outcomes, follow-up work, afterthoughts on the significance of the strategy to pupils' learning and teachers' teaching and reports about experiences with the strategies in different geography classes. The TTG approach fits with the requirements of the National Curriculum in England, where information processing skills, inquiry skills, creative thinking skills, reasoning skills and evaluation skills are required to be taught as part of normal teaching.

Thus, when teachers meet new ideas (initiation), the source needs to be respected and credible. In the novice stage when they are experimenting, someone close at hand who can help with planning and give tips for classroom practice is invaluable. It is not unusual for the teacher to have doubts (the concerns stage) about how the ideas can be scaled up into coherent long-term teaching plans and introduced to colleagues who may not be so keen. This, of course, is when initiatives often falter. Overcoming the doubts (consolidation) is supported by being able to watch others practice, through video or observation, studying for a higher degree, coaching programs, collaborating with other teachers – all of which allow the opportunity for social learning. Once teachers become more confident, they begin to make connections with other educational agendas and they want to influence school policies (expansion). Finally, some teachers benefit from the opportunity to share their experience with others through writing or speaking at conferences (commitment). This process crystallizes their personal growth and helps them reflect on their change in their self-concept as an educator.

Examples of Thinking Through Geography Activities

Most students enjoy TTG strategies like Odd One Out, Mysteries, Reading Photographs, Fact or Opinion and Living Graphs.

An example of a very simple but effective strategy is Odd One Out. Like all strategies it can be used across a wide spectrum of ages and ability ranges (and even subjects) with only small changes. We present here a version of Odd One Out (next paragraph) (Leat & Nichols, 2000) designed for a geography lesson about natural disasters in vocational schools for pupils 12–13 years of age. The major concept being addressed by Odd One Out is classification. The strategy uses a very simple format in asking students to pick the odd one out from a list of words. It can be used at the beginning of the lesson to probe pupils' existing understanding or perhaps more effectively halfway through or at the end to assess the learning. Debriefing is very important, for it allows pupils to express different views. In this case some students will come up with cause-effect relations and others will think in terms of geographical zoning. Both show developing understanding of the topic and each gives food for discussion and thought.

Odd One Out

Assignment: Working with your partner look at the set of numbers below, which matches to a word from the list on the word sheet. Pick out the words and write them in your book. Then try to decide which word from each set is the Odd One Out. Underline this word in your book and explain why it is the Odd One Out and what the other two have in common.

Word sheet: 1 Hurricane, 2 Lava, 3 Dry, 4 Rainforest, 5 Earthquake, 6 Desert, 7 Flooding, 8 Volcano, 9 Equator, 10 Magma

Set of numbers: Set A: 1-2-10, Set B: 4-8-9, Set C: 6-7-3, Set D: 5-2-7, Set E: 7-1-9

Alternatively:

Below you see a set of four geographical words or concepts. Decide which is the Odd One Out and why. In every assignment there is more than one option. Do not use an atlas, wall map or computer. Note down two answers for every assignment. Describe what connects the other three.

- ♦ Bucharest is the Odd One Out because . . . .
- ♦ Buenos Aires is the Odd One Out because . . . .
- ♦ Santiago is the Odd One Out because . . . .
- ♦ Amazon is the Odd One Out because . . ..
- ➢ Deforestation is the Odd One Out because. . . ..
- ➢ Beach is the Odd One Out because . . . .
- ➢ Mountain slope is the Odd One Out because . .. .
- ➢ Erosion is the Odd One Out because . . . .

Next, imagine a family with two parents and some children. One of the parents can get an attractive job with a higher salary in another part of the country. The task is to choose a new residence for the family. Students receive a text about the preferences of family members, a selection of advertisements from real estate agents and an atlas. After a small-group discussion, a plenary discussion takes place. The geographical key concepts of place and spatial interaction are present. Students can use concepts like urban, rural, location, distance, mobility and accessibility. Furthermore, they must use maps to locate the possible residences and to compare the locations.

The result is an overview of situational characteristics of the residences offered, including the location and the accessibility to other facilities important for the family. Efficient problem solving requires metacognitive thinking about selecting an adequate strategy including an orientation on possible activities and their sequence. It also means that students are willing to use exploratory talk in the sense of talk in which partners engage critically but constructively with each other's ideas. The task can be enhanced by inviting examination of the reliability of sources: What is the interest of house sellers and estate agents offering information? After finishing the task, students should be able to reflect on the problem-solving strategies used and the practicability of the approach for solving other geographical assignments.

In the Mystery Method, stories that end in key questions are used to lead into the presentation of a problem or question. In small groups, the students try to resolve these questions by gathering together index cards with uncategorized information (e.g., text cards, statistics, pictures, maps) into a case study. Thus, effect associations are portrayed in the examined subject areas with cards and arrows. Depending on the students and choice of point of view and the emphasis of individual aspects, various different results are possible. The recognition of this is one of the main goals and is viewed as a skill acquisition. In all sub-phases of the development, the aim is the application of geography-specific working practices and skills.

The students of their own accord select the following central aspects of the Mystery Method as a teaching method in different passages and point out the qualities of the dilemma debate. The methods allow the examination, analysis and discussion of complex systems of worldly phenomena in the manner of speaking to each other and the manner of taking into account information; system associations, partial aspects of the systems and the whole system; meanings are assigned, meanings come about in the debate with each other and can remain with the subject as the respective individual opinions; the recognition that a whole system can be coherent in itself despite different viewpoints is enabled; the acquisition of own opinions creates opinion and judgment reference points for complex systems of worldly phenomena; and social forms of learning support learning processes, if they favor individual participation and enjoyment in the exchange, content and methodology are connected by an association of meaning.

Training for Thinking Through Geography

Information about the forms of workshops for teachers is rather limited, perhaps because many different varieties were tried. Leat's ten roles for teachers are obviously relevant. Videotapes played an important part in in-service training. Where research is summarizing or generalizing from classroom observation, then the opportunity to relate the general to a particular instance is part of the process of making sense. Where research has an applied focus, then providing a mental picture of the action described is critical to many observers and puts flesh on the bones of the generalization.

Extensions of Thinking Through Geography

In England it is interesting that the TTG strategies are being increasingly adapted by teachers in other subjects, notably history, religious education, music, design, modern foreign languages and English. TTG has spread to the Netherlands, Germany and Norway.

References and Bibliography

Applis, S. (2016). Geography teachers' concepts of working with Thinking Through Geography strategies: Results of an empirical reconstructive study. *International Research in Geographical and Environmental Education*, 25(3), 195–210. https://doi.org/10.1080/10382046.2016.1155326

Cox, M., Elen, J., & Steegen, A. (2020). Systems thinking in geography: Can high school students do it? *International Research in Geographical and Environmental Education*, *28*(1), 37–52. https://doi.org/10.1080/10382046.2017.1386413

Hooghuis, F., van der Schee, J., van der Velde, M., Imants, J., & Volman, M. (2014). The adoption of Thinking Through Geography strategies and their impact on teaching geographical reasoning in Dutch secondary schools. *International Research in Geographical and Environmental Education*, *23*(3), 242–258. https://doi.org/10.1080/10382046.2014.927168

Leat, D. (2001). *Thinking Through Geography* (second edition). Cambridge: Chris Kington.

Leat, D. (2002). Thinking Through Geography. In M. Smith (Ed.), *Aspects of teaching secondary geography: Perspectives on practice* (pp. 109–117). London & New York: The Open University.

Leat, D., & Lin, M. (2003). Developing a pedagogy for metacognition and transfer: Some signposts for the generation and use of knowledge and the creation of research partnerships. *British Educational Research Journal*, *29*(3), 383–414. https://doi.org/10.1080/0141192031000156015

Leat, D., & Nichols, A. (2000). Observing pupils' mental strategies: Signposts for scaffolding. *International Research in Geographical and Environmental Education*, *9*(1), 19–35. https://doi.org/10.1080/10382040008667627

Leat, D., van der Schee, J., & Vankan, L. (2005). New strategies for learning geography: A tool for teachers' professional development in England and the Netherlands. *European Journal of Teacher Education*, *28*(3), 327–342. https://doi.org/10.1080/02619760500269483

Nichols, A., & Kinninment, D. (2001). *More Thinking Through Geography*. Cambridge: Chris Kington.

Nichols, A., Kinninment, D., & Leat, D. (2005). *More Thinking Through Geography* (second edition). Cambridge: Chris Kington.

van der Schee, J. (2020). Thinking Through Geography in times of the COVID-19 pandemic. *J-READING: Journal of Research and Didactics in Geography*, *2*(9), 21–30. https://doi.org/10.4458/3617-0

van der Schee, J., Leat, D., & Vankan, L. (2006). Effects of the use of Thinking Through Geography strategies. *International Research in Geographical and Environmental Education*, *15*(2), 124–133. https://doi.org/10.2167/irgee190.0

van der Schee, J., Vankan, L. & Leat, D. (2003). The international challenge of more Thinking Through Geography. *International Research in Geographical and Environmental Education*, *12*(4), 330–343. https://doi.org/10.1080/10382040308667545

Section B

Programs Across the Traditional Curriculum

Some programs can be used in virtually any subject and are subject-content free. We review the best known and best evaluated in this section.

6

Reciprocal Teaching (RT)

The concept of Reciprocal Teaching was reported in 1984 in a classic paper by Annemarie Palincsar and Ann Brown. It is based on four major comprehension skills – predicting, summarizing, questioning and clarifying. Each of these is modeled by the teacher through dialogue. Students/pupils are given the opportunity to practice using each skill prior to running their own reciprocal reading group. The meaning of the text is jointly constructed through discussion between all group members. An appointed group leader prompts discussion for each of the strategies, so that all students are given the opportunity to apply and refine their skills when predicting, clarifying, questioning and summarizing.

RT utilizes the strategy of prediction, whereby students/pupils predict before reading and then use those predictions during reading to check if they are correct. Students then move on to clarifying things they do not understand by asking the teacher questions, or having the teacher ask questions during reading, in order to clarify difficult sections of text or point out areas where students should pay particular attention. After the text is read, questions are asked of a student or a group of students to enhance retention and check how much was learned. Finally, comprehension is achieved by engaging the students in a summary of either a page or the entire text selection of what they just read. The teacher supports the students by rephrasing or elaborating on their answers, statements and questions.

Although originally focused on reading comprehension, RT has been extended into mathematics, science and social studies.

Effects of Reciprocal Teaching

The classic study of RT by Palincsar and Brown (1984) (with alternative treatment and two control groups) found that RT led to a significant improvement in the quality of the summaries and questions, sizable gains on criterion-referenced tests of comprehension, reliable maintenance over time, generalization to classroom comprehension tests, transfer to novel tasks that tapped the trained skills and improvement in standardized comprehension scores. RT was both comprehension-fostering and comprehension-monitoring. Brown and Palincsar (1985) compared RT to teacher direct instruction and teacher modeling of the four strategies, finding that all groups improved but the RT group improved most. In another study they demonstrated that isolated skills practice did not yield gains compared to RT. They also found that RT was more effective than summarizing or questioning alone.

There has been one major review of RT (Rosenshine and Meister, 1994), who reviewed 16 studies, which include four journal articles and unpublished studies indexed in Dissertation Abstracts International or conference papers (12). As dissertations typically have less significant results than journal papers, the findings may under-estimate effects. When standardized tests were used to assess comprehension, the median effect size favoring RT was 0.32. When experimenter-developed comprehension tests were used, the median effect size was 0.88.

In seven studies, the investigators trained classroom teachers to provide RT instruction to students and the investigators assessed the level of teacher performance in five of these. Teacher implementation was reported as high in four of these. There was little direct observation of the quality of the RT dialogue in these studies and no investigator presented a set of criteria specifically designed for evaluating reciprocal teaching. The number of instructional sessions provided in these studies ranged from 6 to 100. There was no relationship between the size of the instructional group and the significance of the results. After eliminating studies using only standardized tests, group size varied from 2 to 23 students.

A further relevant review by Rosenshine et al. (1996) focused on teaching students to generate questions. A cognitive strategy is a heuristic. That is, a cognitive strategy is not a direct procedure or an algorithm to be followed precisely, but rather a guide that serves to support learners as they develop internal procedures that enable them to perform higher-level operations. Generating questions about material that is read is an example of a cognitive strategy. Generating questions does not lead directly, in a step-by-step manner, to comprehension. Rather, in the process of generating questions, students need to search the text and combine information and these processes help students comprehend what they read.

A total of 26 studies met the inclusion criteria, 9 of which were RT studies, included because they showed that during the RT dialogues at least 75% of the time was spent asking and responding to questions. The authors explored results for five different procedural prompts: (a) signal words for starting questions, such as who, what, where, when, why and how, (b) generic question stems and generic questions, (c) the main idea of a passage, (d) question types and (e) story grammar categories.

For standardized tests, the median effect size was 0.36, but 0.87 for the 16 studies that used experimenter-developed comprehension tests and 0.85 for the five studies that used a summarization test. Which prompts were most effective? When standardized tests were used and we consider only those prompts used in three or more studies, then signal words were the most effective prompt (median effect size = 0.36). Results were notably lower when the question type prompt or no prompt was used. When experimenter-developed comprehension tests were used, generic questions or question stems and signal words were the most effective prompts.

The National Institute of Child Health and Human Development (2000) found a further 11 studies on reciprocal teaching.

These studies covered grades 1–6 and tended to use more strategies – seven had combinations of summarizing, questioning, clarifying and prediction and added either monitoring or collaborative learning Four studies reported improvements on experimenter tests and three improvements on standardized tests, consistent with Rosenshine and Meister (1994).

More recently, the Education Endowment Foundation (2019) in the UK has conducted a trial of RT involving 98 schools and 5,222 pupils (testing a whole-class approach with 8–9-year-olds) and a targeted approach for students struggling with reading comprehension aged 9–11) (where teachers worked with groups of six children). Sessions were delivered for 20 – 30 minutes at least once per week in the universal intervention and at least twice per week in the targeted intervention, for a minimum of 12 weeks.

Children in the targeted intervention group made the equivalent of two additional months' progress in both primary outcomes (overall reading and reading comprehension) on average, compared to equivalent children in other schools. Children in the targeted intervention also made more progress in both secondary outcomes (reading accuracy and pupil comprehension meta-cognition), while the universal intervention showed effects for only pupil comprehension meta-cognition. Among children receiving free school meals (FSM), analysis again showed an effect on reading comprehension for pupils in the targeted intervention and universal version.

Theoretical Underpinnings of Reciprocal Teaching

Brown and Palincsar (1989) note that RT was supported by three related theories of guided learning: Vygotsky's zone of proximal development (Vygotsky, 1978), proleptic teaching (or teaching "in anticipation of competence") (Rogoff & Gardner, 1984) and expert scaffolding (Wood, Bruner, & Ross, 1976). Collins (1990) also noted that RT was an example of "cognitive apprenticeship", in which novices are taught the processes that experts use to handle complex tasks.

The experts begin by modeling the task for the child. Then they assist the child and gradually cede more and more responsibility to the child until the child can do the task independently. Brown and Palincsar (1989) present the idea of *expert scaffolding*. In this, the expert acts as a guide, shaping the learning efforts of the novices and providing support for the learning until it is no longer needed. The metaphor of a scaffold captures the idea of an adjustable and temporary support that can be removed when no longer necessary. The first use of the term "scaffolding" was by Wood et al. (1976) to refer to the instructional process whereby an adult controls "those elements of the task that are initially beyond the learner's capacity, thus permitting the learner to concentrate upon and complete only those elements that are within his range of competence" (p. 90).

Theory justified research on question generation, noting that it was a means of providing active processing, central focusing, and other comprehension-fostering and comprehension-monitoring activities. However, no theory was provided to justify using specific procedural prompts. In any case, the theoretical rationale for studying question generation does not provide a teacher with specific information on how to develop prompts or how to teach question generation. Consequently, investigators developed or selected a variety of different prompts, including signal words, generic question stems and generic questions, the main idea of a passage, question types and story grammar categories.

Structure and Implementation of Reciprocal Teaching

Palincsar and Brown (1984) noted that training studies that (1) forced the student to be active, (2) provided feedback in the utility of that action and (3) provided instruction in why, when, and where such activities should be applied had been much more successful in inducing transfer. Brown and Palincsar (1985) found that RT was effective even when introduced with non-volunteer teachers and operated in a whole class setting, and when generalized to science and mathematics classes (this was confirmed by Kelly et al., 1994). They had always regarded RT as a form of general education in thinking critically rather than a specific form of reading instruction.

RT refers to learning conditions in which children "first experience a particular set of cognitive activities in the presence of experts, and gradually come to perform these functions by themselves" (Brown & Palincsar, 1989, p. 123). In RT, (a) the focus is upon teaching students specific, concrete, comprehension-fostering strategies that they can apply to the reading of new text and (b) this instruction takes place primarily in the context of a dialogue between the teacher and the students.

Students read a passage of expository material, paragraph by paragraph. During the reading they learn and practice four reading comprehension strategies: generating questions, summarizing, attempting to clarify word meanings or confusing text and predicting what might appear in the next paragraph. During the early stages of reciprocal teaching, the teacher assumes the major responsibility for instruction by overtly, explicitly and concretely modeling the process of using these strategies on a selection of text. After the teacher has modeled, the students practice the strategies on the next section of text and the teacher supports each student's participation through specific feedback, additional modeling, coaching, hints and explanation. The teacher adjusts the difficulty of the task according to the current level of the student, as described by Palincsar and Brown (1984):

> The teacher models and explains, relinquishing part of the task to novices only at the level each one is capable of negotiating at any one time. Increasingly, as the novice becomes more competent, the teacher increases her demands, requiring participation at a slightly more challenging level.
>
> (p. 13)

During this guided practice, the teacher invites students to initiate discussion and to react to other students' statements. Students' participation can include (a) elaborating or commenting on another student's summary, (b) suggesting other questions,

(c) commenting on another's predictions (d) requesting clarification of material they did not understand and (e) helping to resolve misunderstandings.

The teacher supports students by rephrasing or elaborating on their answers, statements and questions. In the course of this guided practice, there is a gradual shift in responsibility from the teacher doing much of the work to the child taking over the major thinking role, while the teacher observes and helps only when needed. At this point, the practice becomes a dialogue: one student asks questions, another answers and a third comments on the answer; one student summarizes and another comments on or helps to improve the summary; one student identifies a difficult word and the other students help to infer the meaning and give reasons for the inferences they made. The emphasis throughout is on cooperative effort by teacher and students to bring meaning to the ideas in the text, rather than merely restating the words. In addition, during the dialogue, students are provided instruction in why, when and where such activities should be applied to new text. In reciprocal teaching, much emphasis is placed on encouraging students to provide instructional support for each other.

Then, after some practice, each student takes a turn at modeling the strategies and leading the discussion. Gradually, the teacher's role fades into the background. Clearly, managing such a curriculum requires very specific pedagogical skills and places a high demand on the teacher, not least in dealing subtly with dialogue off task and misconceptions.

Implementation integrity of RT has been established using an ISL Observational Checklist developed by Paris et al. (1984), which includes 12 teaching behaviors:

(1) Gains students' attention
(2) Introduces lesson
(3) States goals
(4) Reviews previous information
(5) Informs students about (a) what it is, (b) how it works, and (c) when to use and when not to use
(6) Encourages metaphorical reasoning

(7) Persuades why strategy is useful
(8) Models and demonstrates strategy
(9) Allows immediate practice
(10) Provides praise and corrective feedback
(11) Fades support
(12) Bridges to other reading/learning.

Somewhat similarly, Rosenshine and Meister (1994) provide a criteria checklist for quality of reciprocal teaching:

1. Students are instructed in a repertoire of strategies (two or more) that they can use to help them better understand what they read.
2. Teacher models each of the activities.
3. Students are invited to make comments regarding the modeling and the passage, such as, "Was there more important information?" or "Does anyone have anything more to add to my prediction?"
4. Students are provided with guided assistance as they participate at whatever level they are capable in carrying out the strategies.
5. Teacher supports each child's participation in the dialogue through specific feedback, praise, prompting, additional modeling, paraphrases, coaching, hints and explanation.
6. Teacher invites students to initiate discussion and to react to other students' statements. Such participation can include (a) suggesting other questions, (b) elaborating upon a summary, (c) commenting on another's predictions, (d) requesting clarification of material they did not understand, (e) offering additional comments on the content and (f) helping to resolve misunderstandings.
7. During RT, there is a gradual shift from the teacher doing much of the work to the child taking over the major thinking role. The teacher gradually transfers control of the dialogues to the students and becomes a supportive observer.
8. During the dialogues, instruction is provided on why, where and when these strategies might be applied.

Later, Palincsar and her associates attempted to describe the important instructional features of dialogues by comparing the dialogues of several primary teachers. They found that the less successful teachers often merely recited information about the strategy being taught during the dialogues. Students' involvement occurred mostly at the word level; they were asked only to provide labels for strategies or to complete sentences begun by the teacher. In contrast, the more successful teachers engaged students at the "idea" level and focused the dialogue on using the strategies when discussing a passage. They encouraged students to engage in the dialogue by rephrasing questions when students were unable to respond and by using and elaborating upon other students" responses. They provided support by explicitly modeling strategies ("If I were asking a question, I …"; "If I were going to summarize, I …") and helped students label the language or features of the interaction.

Examples of RT Activities

The following example (courtesy of Annemarie Palincsar) illustrates how the teacher solicits student responses and provides prompts, models, cues and feedback regarding the use of cognitive strategies during the dialogues:

> **Student 1:** My question is, what does the aquanaut need when he goes under water?
> **Student 2:** A watch.
> **Student 3:** Flippers.
> **Student 4:** A belt.
> **Student 1:** Those are all good answers.
> **Teacher:** Nice job! I have a question too. Why does the aquanaut wear a belt? What is so special about it?
> **Student 3:** It's a heavy belt and keeps him from floating up to the top again.
> **Teacher:** Good for you.
> **Student 1:** For my summary now: This paragraph was about what aquanauts need to take when they go under the water.

Student 5: And also about why they need those things.
Student 3: I think we need to clarify gear.
Student 6: That's the special things they need.
Teacher: Another word for gear in this story might be equipment, the equipment that makes it easier for the aquanauts to do their job.
Student 1: I don't think I have a prediction to make.
Teacher: Well, in the story they tell us that there are "many strange and wonderful creatures" that the aquanauts see as they do their work. My prediction is that they'll describe some of these creatures. What are some of the strange creatures you already know about that live in the ocean?
Student 6: Octopuses.
Student 3: Whales?
Student 5: Sharks!
Teacher: Let's listen and find out. Who'll be our teacher?

As the dialogue continues, students in the group progressively take on more responsibility for carrying out the dialogue. Students in the group begin to provide models, hints and prompts to each other, as well as feedback regarding the use of the strategies. Although the teacher is not absent from these later discussions, the role of the teacher shifts to that of a sympathetic coach.

A development of RT was reported in subsequent studies. In these, students were first introduced to the four strategies during three to six traditional lessons that were conducted *before* the dialogues began. These lessons were developed to introduce the students to the "language" of RT by providing direct instruction in each strategy. Separate lessons were devoted to instruction in question generation, summarization, clarification and prediction.

Training for Reciprocal Teaching

The original training described by Brown and Palincsar (1985) involved three spaced sessions (of unknown length) involving video demonstration and practice, then guided practice with a group of children including sample scripts and questions and weekly follow-up. With larger groups of students, the transfer to peer-led dialogue tended to be quicker.

In the UK, training for RT has been done by the Fischer Family Trust (https://fft.org.uk/literacy/reciprocal-reading/), lasting for one academic year. There were two days of initial training (one in advance of program delivery), with three half days in-school support visits thereafter, supported by teacher manuals and pupil books. Dandelion Learning (https://www.dandelionlearning.co.uk/reciprocal-reading-online-training/) also offers training. Highland Literacy (https://highlandliteracy.com/reciprocal-reading/) has a free downloadable PowerPoint, instruction leaflet and cue cards (https://highlandliteracy.files.wordpress.com/2018/02/reciprocal-reading/).

A search of the internet for "reciprocal teaching" *or* "reciprocal reading" *and* "training" *or* "professional development" should yield dividends.

Extensions of RT

As mentioned earlier, RT has now been applied not only in reading comprehension, but also in mathematics, science and social studies. RT can now also be found in colleges and universities. Furthermore, it has spread round the world, and many recent reports are from countries where the native language is not English. Thus, there are published reports from Nigeria, Palestine and Thailand on RT in science up to 2022 and on mathematics in Pakistan up to 2021. There are also studies of RT with English as a Foreign Language students from India, Iran and Thailand up to 2022. A report from Germany used RT with Self-Regulated Learning (SRL), showing SRL added a further improvement.

References and Bibliography

Brown, A. L., & Palincsar, A. S. (1985). *Reciprocal teaching of comprehension strategies: A natural history of one program for enhancing learning.* Technical Report No. 334. Cambridge, MA: Bolt, Beranek and Newman, Inc. ERIC ED 257 046.

Brown, A. L., & Palincsar, A. S. (1989). Guided, cooperative learning and individual knowledge acquisition. In L. B. Resnick (Ed.), *Knowing, learning, and instruction: Essays in honor of robert glaser* (pp. 393–451). Hillsdale, NJ: Erlbaum.

Collins, A., Brown, J. S., & Newman, S. E. (1990). Cognitive apprenticeship: Teaching the crafts of reading, writing, and mathematics. In L. Resnick (Ed.), *Knowing, learning, and instruction: Essays in honor of Robert Glaser* (pp. 453–494). Hillsdale, NJ: Erlbaum.

Education Endowment Foundation (2019). *Reciprocal Reading: Evaluation report*. London: EEF. https://d2tic4wvo1iusb.cloudfront.net/documents/projects/Reciprocal_Reading.pdf?v=1682074239

Kelly, M., Moore, D. W., & Tuck, B. F. (1994). Reciprocal teaching in a regular primary school classroom. *Journal of Educational Research*, *88*(1), 53–61. https://doi.org/10.1080/00220671.1994.9944834

National Institute of Child Health and Human Development (2000). Report of the National Reading Panel. *Teaching children to read: An evidence-based assessment of the scientific research literature on reading and its implications for reading instruction: Reports of the subgroups* (NIH Publication No. 00-4754). Washington, DC: U.S. Government Printing Office.

Palincsar, A. S., & Brown, A. L. (1984). Reciprocal teaching comprehension-fostering and comprehension-monitoring activities. *Cognition and Instruction*, *1*(2), 117–175. https://doi.org/10.1207/s1532690xci0102_1

Palincsar, A. S., & Brown, A. L. (1986). Interactive teaching to promote independent learning from text. *The Reading Teacher*, *39*(8), 771–777. https://www.jstor.org/stable/20199221

Paris, S. C., Cross, D. R., & Lipson, M. Y. (1984). Informed strategies for learning: A program to improve children's reading awareness and comprehension. *Journal of Educational Psychology*, *76*(6), 1239–1252. https://doi.org/10.1037/0022-0663.76.6.1239

Rogoff, B., & Gardner, W. P. (1984). Adult guidance of cognitive development. In B. Rogoff, & J. Lave (Eds.), *Everyday cognition: Its development in social context* (pp. 95–116). Cambridge, MA: Harvard University Press.

Rosenshine, B., & Meister, C. (1994). Reciprocal teaching: A review of the research. *Review of Educational Research*, *64*(4), 479–530. https://doi.org/10.3102/00346543064004479

Rosenshine, B., Meister, C., & Chapman, S. (1996). Teaching students to generate questions: A review of the intervention studies. *Review of Educational Research*, *66*(2), 181–221. https://doi.org/10.3102/00346543066002181

Vygotsky, L. S. (1978). *Mind in society: The development of higher psychological processes.* Cambridge, MA: Harvard University Press.

Wood, D. J., Bruner, J. S., & Ross, G. (1976). The role of tutoring in problem solving. *Journal of Child Psychology and Psychiatry*, *17*(2), 89–100. https://doi.org/10.1111/j.1469-7610.1976.tb00381.x

Activating Children's Thinking Skills (ACTS)

ACTS is a methodology for enhancing thinking skills across the curriculum, adopting an "infusion" methodology. An infusion approach seeks to identify contexts across the curriculum where particular thinking skills can be developed; for example, causal reasoning in a science lesson, classification of mathematical shapes, decision-making with reference to personal decisions or to fictional/historical characters. The benefits of infusion are seen as: matching thinking skills directly with topics in the curriculum; invigorating content instruction leading to deeper understanding; using classroom time optimally; directly supporting teaching for thoughtfulness across the curriculum; and facilitating transfer and reinforcement of learning. The approach seems particularly appropriate for the elementary/primary level, where the teacher is in charge of almost the whole curriculum in a classroom. However, the method is not confined to the elementary/primary level and has since been successfully adopted at post-primary level.

ACTS is associated with the name of Carol McGuiness, Professor of Psychology at Queen's University, Belfast, Northern Ireland. She directed the Activating Children's Thinking (ACTS) project in Northern Ireland, which used an infusion methodology for enhancing children's thinking across the curriculum.

She developed ACTS starting around 2000. It has since influenced work in all regions of the UK and overseas.

Effects of Activating Children's Thinking Skills

The early evaluative research involved only feedback of teacher perceptions. Initially teachers struggled to find time and ACTS lessons went on for longer than planned, so the teachers had to be ready to allow time for student thinking and not jump in with ready-made answers. However, all teachers felt ACTS had enhanced their professional development. Even in a short time they were able to see benefits for the children's thinking, their own teaching and the classroom in general. However, these subjective perceptions were insufficient for a proper evaluation.

In 2005, McGuiness et al. reported on the pattern of change over three years in children's self-ratings on three Assessment of Learner-Centered Practices (ALCPS) scales, derived from the American Psychological Association's Learner-Centered Principles – Active Learning Strategies, Effort Avoidance Strategies and Work Avoidance Goals. Sample items scale are: "I spend some time thinking about how to do my work before I begin it" (planning), "I ask myself questions while I do my work to make sure I understand" (self-monitoring), "When I make mistakes, I try to figure out why" (evaluating). However, the number of ACTS intervened children was not reported. The control group was a representative sample of children in the last three years of their primary schooling ($n = 548$).

All ability groups reported that they used active learning strategies less often as they progressed through school. For the lowest ability children, the drop off was the most severe. Scores for boys and girls were very similar, but the scores for boys were generally lower. Analysis showed that, controlling for the effects of other variables (sex, age, free school meals), participating in the ACTS intervention for three years had a positive effect on children's ratings of their use of cognitive and metacognitive strategies, in the sense that it moderated decreases that were evident in the control group. However, there was no effect of ACTS on low ability groups. The effect was confined to those children who had participated in ACTS for three years; participating for one or two years did not seem to be sufficient.

McGuinness et al. (2007) reported a longitudinal evaluation of ACTS, evaluating enhancements in 8–11-year-old children's thinking and learning and the effects on both pupils' and teachers' learning. One hundred and thirty-four teachers participated in five ACTS professional development days over the school year. During that time teachers planned, designed and taught infusion thinking lessons. In the main intervention study, comparisons were made between three groups of children. Two groups of children participated in ACTS for different lengths of time: one group for three years ($N = 292$, 12 classes) and another group for one or two years ($N = 412$, 17 classes). Children from these ACTS classes were compared with a third group of similar children from different schools who were not taught using the ACTS pedagogy ($N = 548$, 25 classes). The children's learning from all groups was tracked longitudinally over three years.

Measures were more learner-centered than was usual: a suite of self-assessment inventories, the Assessment of Learner-Centered Practices (ALCPs). Seven scales enabled pupils to evaluate their learning (rated on a four-point Likert scale) with regard to a range of cognitive and motivational constructs: Active Learning Strategies, Knowledge Seeking Curiosity, Task Mastery, Performance-Oriented Goals, Effort Avoidance Strategies, Work Avoidance Goals and Self-Efficacy. The scales showed good internal reliabilities for the sample at all ages (0.57–0.86, the vast majority over 0.75). Separate analyses were carried out on Low, Moderate and High Ability groups.

Participating in ACTS had a statistically significant positive effect on how children rated themselves with regard to their use of cognitive and metacognitive strategies, their willingness to work harder and to put in more effort. However, the pattern of change took time to build and those children who participated in ACTS for three years benefited most. In addition, moderate to high ability children (who represented 80% of the sample) benefited most. No positive outcomes were identified for lower ability children, at least on these self-rating measures. All of the self-rating measures were significantly correlated with measures of attainment in reading and mathematics, but these effects were small. Teachers experienced changes in their images of themselves as teachers. They described an increased awareness of the importance and value of teaching thinking, of being more open to alternative approaches and allowing children to be more independent in their learning.

Turning now to an evaluation published in a peer reviewed journal, Dewey and Bento (2009) evaluated ACTS in relation to the cognitive, social and emotional development of 404 children aged 8–11 in eight volunteer elementary schools, randomly allocated to 160 in the experimental group and 244 in the waiting list control group. At pre-test there were no statistically significant differences between groups in terms of gender, age, ethnicity and level of special educational need. In total 26 teachers delivered the intervention (24 females and two males).

Pre-, post- and delayed post-tests were used to investigate changes in children's cognitive abilities, self-perceptions and social/behavioral skills. The Cognitive Abilities Test is a multiple-choice test that assesses general reasoning abilities and a pupil's capacity to apply these to verbal, quantitative and non-verbal cognitive tasks, divided into three batteries namely verbal, quantitative and non-verbal. The Myself–As–A–Learner Scale (MALS) examines children's self-perceptions as learners, consisting of 20 self-referring statements on which students rate themselves on a five-point scale. The Taxonomy of Problematic Social Situations (TOPS) is a questionnaire that teachers complete to identify the specific social situations or tasks a particular pupil finds difficult. The teacher is asked whether the child experiences difficulties in 44 problematic social situations and rates the child on a five-point scale.

Teachers received training in ACTS, involving two days' initial training focusing on the taxonomy of thinking and infusion lesson design, techniques of thinking diagrams and thinking groups. Two review days focusing on metacognition, language and social collaboration followed. Treatment fidelity checks occurred half-termly. The experimental group made significantly greater gains in cognitive ability skills over a two-year period compared to controls. The effect size was partial $\eta^2 = 0.02$, which would be described as between small and medium, but is a good outcome for a large-scale study of this type. Between subjects a small to medium effect size ($\eta^2 = 0.03$) was noted for impact across individual pupils. There were no significant positive changes on MALS or TOPS. Qualitative data demonstrated a positive impact on children's social and emotional development. In addition, teacher professional development was reported to be enhanced.

Theoretical Underpinnings of Activating Children's Thinking Skills

Maximizing transfer of thinking and learning beyond the immediate context in which it was learned is the heart of the matter. All cognitive interventions have risks in this regard. Separate programs risk not transferring to the school curriculum. Interventions confined to one area of the curriculum might not generalize to other subjects. Infusing thinking across the curriculum runs its own risks – it may get lost in the midst of subject-knowledge based teaching or pupils may fail to see the connection between similar types of thinking in different subject areas.

The theory underpinning the ACTS approach is based on the principles of infusion from Swartz and Parks (1994) and emphasizes the explicit teaching of thinking within the current curriculum. These authors (in the US) address engaging in complex thinking tasks and provide sample lessons and reproducible materials in the areas of decision making and problem solving. They then focus on understanding, retention and clarifying ideas, providing sample lessons on comparing and contrasting, classification, determining parts and whole relationships, sequencing, finding reasons and conclusions and uncovering assumptions. Then they touch on creative thinking and provide sample lessons on generating possibilities and creating metaphors. After this, there is a focus on critical thinking and sample lessons are provided on determining the reliability of sources, causal explanations, prediction, generalization, reasoning by analogy and conditional reasoning. Swartz & Parks (1994) also use thinking diagrams to depict the different stages in specific thinking skills, alongside thinking groups to support children in the social construction of knowledge. Swartz and Park's book is still available second-hand on Amazon.com, for example.

Beyond this, the ACTS Thinking Framework was derived from a cognitive perspective and acknowledged the importance of metacognition for cognitive development – not only as a product of development but also as potential means for fostering development. Two theoretical shifts were required. The first shift was from considering metacognition as "revealing" cognitive development, to a more constructivist perspective on metacognition as fostering or "creating" development. The second shift acknowledged the power of social learning as a mediator for metacognition, and the perspective shifted to social-constructivism, particularly to the role of classroom dialogue. Hence language and dialogue were of primary interest. Finally, the ultimate goal was that the ACTS intervention should have an impact on children's capacity to manage their own thinking – to think independently – and the concept of metacognition was linked within a broader cognitive-motivational framework of self-regulation.

Structure and Implementation of Activating Children's Thinking Skills

An infusion approach seeks to identify contexts across the curriculum where particular thinking skills can be developed; for example, causal reasoning in a science lesson, classification of mathematical shapes, decision-making with reference to personal decisions or to fictional/historical characters. The benefits of infusion are: matching thinking skills directly with topics in the curriculum; invigorating content instruction leading to deeper understanding; using classroom time optimally; directly supporting teaching for thoughtfulness across the curriculum; and facilitating transfer and reinforcement of learning. Moreover, the approach seems particularly appropriate for primary level, where the teacher is in charge of the whole curriculum in a classroom. However, the method is not confined to primary level and has since been successfully adopted by a group of teachers working in subject areas at post-primary level.

ACTS uses thinking diagrams (or graphic organizers or concept maps) to help make the steps in thinking explicit. For example, a thinking diagram for decision-making invites the students to consider and write down all the options which might be related to the decision (suspending judgment at this stage), then taking each option in turn, weighing the pros and cons of each, before finally deciding on a course of action (see the example later in this chapter). The decisions of historical or literary figures can be evaluated in this way. Such diagrams help organize thinking and slow it to an orderly pace, as well as provide evidence of the process followed. Thinking vocabularies are developed by talking about thinking (which requires the teacher to make time available), the teacher's questioning techniques are developed, and reflection and discussion are important ways to build competence. Teaching also needs to explicitly focus on transfer.

The ACTS thinking framework features a range of different types of thinking, including pattern-making through analyzing wholes and parts, noting similarities and differences (searching for meaning); making predictions and justifying conclusions, reasoning about cause and effect (critical thinking); generating ideas and possibilities, seeing multiple perspectives (creative thinking); solving problems and evaluating solutions (problem-solving); weighing up pros and cons; and making decisions (decision-making). The types of thinking identified in the framework formed the basis for designing infusion lessons.

Searching for Meaning

Searching for Meaning involves sequencing, ordering, ranking, sorting, grouping, classifying, analyzing, identifying parts and wholes, noting similarities and differences, finding patterns and relationships and comparing and contrasting. This group can be characterized as searching out order and imposing meaning on information.

Critical Thinking
Critical thinking involves making predictions and formulating hypotheses, drawing conclusions, giving reasons, distinguishing fact from opinion, determining bias, exploring the reliability of evidence, relating causes and effects, designing a fair test. This group can be characterized as questioning/scrutinizing information and making judgments about it.

Creative Thinking
Creative thinking involves generating ideas and possibilities, brainstorming, building and combining ideas, recognizing and using analogies, formulating one's own point of view, taking multiple perspectives, seeing other points of view.

Decision Making
Decision making involves defining problems, thinking up different solutions, testing solutions, identifying why a decision is necessary, generating options, predicting the likely consequences, weighing up the pros and cons, setting up sub-goals, monitoring progress, deciding on a course of action, reviewing the consequences.

Metacognition
Central to all of the above is metacognition, involving planning, monitoring, evaluating, redirecting.

Examples of Activating Children's Thinking Skills Activities

After some open discussion within the class, the teacher asks students to engage in open brainstorming in their groups to explore what options the country might have for energy sources. She asks them to work together in their groups and record their ideas on a simple graphic organizer, which has Options in the left-hand column and Factors to Consider in the right-hand column. She scaffolds the discussion by making comments like, "Try to think of as many options as you can and write them on your graphic organizers. And talk together about these". Here's a list of options produced by one class, the result of open brainstorming:

> Nuclear
> Coal
> Oil
> Tides
> Lightning
> Geo-thermal
> Wind
> Waves
> Hydroelectric
> Methane Gas
> Natural Gas
> Fracked Gas
> Human Power
> Gravity
> Chemical Reactions

The teacher recognizes that the students have produced a list of a large number of energy sources, some more fanciful than others (though at this stage, all options are treated equally). Trying to decide which one is the best one seems a daunting task. So, she provides more scaffolding: "Let's see if we can think of factors we need to take into account in order to decide which energy source we want to recommend. For example, we should probably consider cost, don't you agree? What else will we want to take into account? Let's make a list of these factors in the next column." Here is the list of factors to consider her students produced:

> Cost to Produce the Energy
> Availability
> Environmental Impact
> Renewability
> Safety
> Cost of the Energy
> Ease of Production

Jobs Lost or Created
Public Acceptability
Technology Needed
Cost to Convert

The students now have a list of things they need to find out about a source of energy to judge how viable it is as the source we should make dominant. So, the teacher asks: "What should we do next?" Many students see that they need to get information about to what degree these factors are present with regard to each energy source and then compare them, before they can make a choice. So, the teacher goes back to the thinking map, which she has posted on the wall. "What is the next question on the thinking map?" Many students repeat the question: "What are the likely consequences of these options?" She continues: "How can we figure out what the consequences of these options are?" The students report that we can project consequences in each of these categories based on information they might be able to get. When she asks for an example about cost, some students respond immediately; for example, they might figure out how much it costs for electricity for their city using solar panels by finding out how much solar panels cost, how many would be needed and how much it costs to install and maintain them.

 The teacher now gives the students an extended matrix as a graphic organizer to use to record and process what they have come up with so far. There is a column for options and a row in which they can record the factors they have identified. She will ask each group to work on just a small number of options from the list, planning to have them record their results on a large chart on which a larger matrix will be drawn so that all of the students can reap the benefits of the work that each team engages in. The chart has little +s and -s, signifying whether the information they have uncovered counts in favor or against the option. It also has *s. Here they are ranking consequences using a two-point scale: more important/less important. Their teacher prompts them to make sure that they have reasons for assigning stars so that if they are challenged, they can defend their judgments.

Training for Activating Children's Thinking Skills

Teachers involved in the first study received training in the ACTS methodology. The model of training involved two days initial training focusing on the taxonomy of thinking and infusion lesson design, the techniques of thinking diagrams and thinking groups and modeling infusion lessons. After this, teachers designed lessons, experimented in their own classrooms, recorded their results and returned the following month to discuss achievements and difficulties and to exchange good practice. Review days then occurred later in the year, focusing on metacognition, language and social collaboration. On these review days, additional thinking skills were introduced, teachers were given feedback and more advanced questioning and teaching-for-transfer skills were discussed.

The training encouraged teachers to identify lessons across the curriculum in which they could teach content alongside a focus on a specific thinking skill. Teachers scripted some of their own lessons. Thus, ACTS did not provide a pre-constructed pack of prescribed lessons, but rather involved training teachers to redesign existing lessons with an explicit thinking skills emphasis. The ACTS Handbook was completed, including 24 lessons illustrating how infusion lessons can be designed and taught over nine different areas, demonstrating ten different thinking strategies (e.g., compare and contrasts, classification, sequencing, prediction, problem solving and decision-making).

Extensions of Activating Children's Thinking Skills

ACTS was originally developed for upper elementary ages but has more general application and has been successfully adapted by groups of teachers working in subject areas at lower secondary and at post-16 level. ACTS has influenced educational developments in Northern Ireland (where it was effectively included in the National Curriculum in 2007), Wales, Scotland and England. It has also been used in Eire and Thailand.

References and Bibliography

Dewey, J., & Bento, J. (2009). Activating Children's Thinking Skills (ACTS): The effects of an infusion approach to teaching thinking in primary schools. *British Journal of Educational Psychology*, *79*, 329–351. doi:10.1348/000709908X344754

McGuiness, C., Curry, C., Eakin, A., & Sheehy, N. (2005). *Thinking lessons for thinking classrooms: Tools for teachers*. London & New York: Routledge.

McGuiness, C., Curry, C., Eakin, A., & Sheehy, N. (2005). *Metacognition in primary classrooms: A pro-ACTive learning effect for children*. Paper given at the ESRC TLRP Annual Conference, 28–30 November 2005, University of Warwick. Metacognition_in_Primary_Classrooms_A_pr20170511-3521-1jhiu0q-libre.pdf (d1wqtxts1xzle7.cloudfront.net)

McGuinness, C., Eakin, A., Curry, C., Sheehy, N., & Bunting, B. (2007). *Building thinking skills in thinking classrooms: ACTS in Northern Ireland*. Paper presented at *the 13th International Conference on Thinking*, June 17–21, 2007, Norrköping, Sweden. http://www.ep.liu.se/ecp/021/vol1 or https://ep.liu.se/ecp/021/vol1/015/ecp2107015.pdf

Swartz, R. J., & Parks, S. (1994). *Infusing the teaching of critical and creative thinking into content instruction: A lesson design handbook for the elementary grades*. Pacific Grove, CA: Critical Thinking Press and Software.

8

Thinking Actively in Social Contexts (TASC)

Thinking Actively in Social Contexts (TASC) is a process model that comprehensively supports fluency, problem solving and reasoning. The essential premise is that all children's learning capacity can be improved through the systematic and coherent teaching of the processes underpinning problem solving and thinking. It is a universal approach that can support all problem solving. Learners are encouraged to: build upon prior knowledge, consider different methods of solution, justify decisions based on reasoning, evaluate their work and reflect on what they are taking away from the activity. All children are capable of thinking and improving their performance. Children need to have a sense of ownership of their learning – they need to be actively involved in the decision-making. The brain thrives on active participation and involvement, and this generates motivation, high self-esteem and confidence. Children need to work collaboratively and co-operatively, to practice their thinking and to share ideas with others.

TASC is based on the work of Belle Wallace and Harvey Adams (see publications 1989 through to 2019) of the Curriculum Development Unit at the University of Natal. Pietermaritzburg, South Africa. It was their opinion that the content of most school subjects was relevant neither to the immediate nor future needs of the prospective citizens of a non-racial South Africa. TASC was developed with black pupils and teachers in KwaZulu/Natal schools. Wallace stayed in South Africa for 15 years during the crumbling of the apartheid regime before returning to the UK.

KwaZulu consists mainly of rural, subsistence farming and low socio-economic urban settlements. TASC was thus developed in and for a challenging environment. The total school enrollment was estimated at 1.5 million in the 1990s (but rapidly rising), with only 67% of the school-age population actually attending school. Moreover, surveys suggested that 53% of the entire population was under 15 years of age. There were high levels of school drop-out, repeating of grades and failure in the Senior Certificate examination – all indicating considerable underachievement. In 1985 only 16% of the year group reached the tenth grade, only 5% passed the Senior Certificate and only 1% gained a level which enabled application for university entrance. Of these latter, few could afford to go to university, and almost all who did were underprepared in academic and other terms, obliging the university to establish bridging courses and student support services.

Although there has been a large increase in spending on education, there is still an acute shortage of teachers. The number of new teachers required is in the tens of thousands, leaving aside the problem of under-qualified teachers currently in posts. At TASC development time in 1986, 13% of teachers in high schools had not even passed Senior Certificate, while 9% had no teaching qualifications at all. There was also a serious shortage of teaching accommodation, with an average class size of 48 pupils in high school.

There were further problems. Firstly, although the pupils' mother tongue and home language were Zulu, English was used as the medium of instruction for all subjects beyond second grade. Inadequacies in the teaching and learning of English compounded the other difficulties experienced by pupils. Many teachers had only a basic command of English and an equally basic understanding of their subject matter. Secondly, large class sizes and a wide range of pupil ability within classes led many teachers to adopt a rigid and didactic teaching style aimed at rote learning of material. This was reinforced by frequent and rigid tests – examinations which required only recall of information. Moreover, the traditional Zulu culture promoted deep respect for senior members of the community and for those in authority. Young people were not encouraged to question their elders and it was considered impolite to push oneself forward as an individual. Social cohesion was strong and consciousness of one's place in society was both implicitly and explicitly encouraged. Some teachers used corporal punishment when pupils ventured to ask questions.

There were also conflicting peer-group identities based on political, social and economic differences and frequent outbreaks of violence in schools as pupils sought to defend and justify their differences. Moreover, because many parents worked away from home for extended periods, children were often cared for by elderly grandparents or relatives who had received little formal education. A great number of students were themselves carers of their younger brothers and sisters, and students had the responsibilities after school of fetching water and wood and cooking.

Thus, little attention was given to analytical, evaluative or creative thinking or to the application of knowledge in problem-solving. The content overload of most syllabuses prevented even the most skilled and creative teachers from developing pupils' active thinking rather than just memorization. These problems put the complaints of the Western countries' education systems into perspective.

Effects of Thinking Actively in Social Contexts

The aims of TASC at the outset were to improve attitudes to school and motivation for learning; improve scholars' self-concepts; help pupils to tackle problems at home, at school or elsewhere that inhibited their school attendance, performance at school, or study outside school; improve scholastic achievement, thereby opening doors for further education or training and employment; equip pupils for decision making and leadership roles in the community and in spheres of industry, commerce and the public service; equip pupils for their future roles as citizens in a society undergoing rapid change; help disadvantaged young people to adopt roles in society for which few, if any, role models existed. This represented a rather large evaluation agenda.

The first TASC course, for a selected group of very high achieving 12–13-year-olds pupils in white schools, demonstrated that over a 5-day (25-hour) period, rapid progress could be made and durable changes in performance recorded. A second course, again 25 hours during a 5-day period, was for pupils in a black high school who were high achievers within that school. The outcomes were similar to the first course – rapid learning, high motivation, improvements in self-image and lasting improvements in performance on specified cognitive tasks (fluency of ideas, goal formulation, strategy selection, solution monitoring).

However, evaluation of later courses by the Schools' Psychological Service, teachers, the students and the researchers themselves revealed certain difficulties. Firstly, students not already achieving highly within the school system for whatever reason would need a foundation course in basic thinking and assistance in achieving oral fluency in English. It was also felt that gains made during the course would be rapidly dissipated unless a constant call was made upon the newly acquired skills during the pupils' subject lessons.

A third major pilot course was subsequently run for a full-sized all-ability grade 8 class of 40 pupils in a black high school, over a six-week period with two two-hour sessions after school each week. The approach was highly successful for those pupils already achieving at a relatively high level and with a reasonable command of English. Others progressed at a much slower rate, causing an expansion of the gap between the rapid and the less rapid learners.

The scope of the work was therefore expanded in two directions: Firstly, the first four years of the five years of high school would be included in the program; and secondly, the syllabus of all major school subjects would be examined to identify and develop opportunities for building the use of the newly acquired skills into regular subject lessons. It was also decided to make an urgent start on the basic course for the first year of high school.

This would enable students to be given differentiated courses aimed at overcoming their various "resistances" to "or difficulties in" learning.

The pattern of subsequent evaluation has been varied. There have been several reports from the UK following Wallace's return there, but many of these are descriptive rather than evaluative (e.g., Wallace et al., 2019). However, there have also been several relatively recent more throughgoing evaluations, especially from Indonesia, all of which have been positive.

A study with 73 seventh graders in Jordan (Awwad et al., 2014) used a self-directed learning readiness scale and a self-efficacy scale across an experimental and control group. Analysis of covariance showed statistically significant differences in favor of the experimental group on the self-directed learning readiness scale only. Turning to studies in Indonesia, Wardhani (2018) used TASC in Biology via a four-dimensional model of define, design, develop and disseminate. The developing phase included developing the TASC model and guidelines, with assessment by an expert, and developing a test for limited and expanded trials. The disseminating phase distributed the TASC model and guidelines. The TASC learning model and guidelines were effective in improving higher order thinking skills, as shown by statistically significant differences in pre-post-test gain scores.

Also in Indonesia, Susanto and Suryadarma (2019) used TASC to develop creative thinking in a biology project on the ecology of rice fields, again deploying the define, design, develop and disseminate model to develop a guidance manual for improved practice. A thinking skills test was applied before and after the project. Ninety-two per cent of the TASC students passed the test, when the minimum passing grade was 75%, while the control group showed little change. This result was highly statistically significant. Fauziah et al. (2020) worked with 271 fifth-grade students from nine classes in public elementary schools. The first three experimental classes used TASC during the research, the second three used the Creative Problem-Solving (CPS) model, while the three control classes used direct instruction (DI). Each class applied the learning model for eight meetings.

On pre-post-tests, TASC did significantly better than CPS (effect size 0.67), which did significantly better than DI (effect size 0.28).

Theoretical Underpinnings of Thinking Actively in Social Contexts

Much of TASC is underpinned by Vygotsky, whose notion of the importance of the social interaction elements of education is key. Vygotsky also emphasized the importance of mediation by a more capable other. Capable tutors (parents, teachers, siblings and peers) initiated the child into more complex tasks by supporting and structuring activities and then fading the support so that the child gradually gained mastery. The learner internalizes the concept and thus gains conscious control. The tutor performs the function of providing "scaffolding" until the learner becomes independent. Vygotsky stressed the importance of socio-cultural transmission and intentional mediation of the learner's experience. Where these two processes were inadequate, the learner failed to develop fully effective cognitive functions. Under-functioning resulting from insufficient mediation of learning experiences can be remediated by appropriate intervention.

Sternberg proposed that intelligence consists of three inter-related aspects: (1) the contextual sub-theory in which intelligence is viewed as mental activity directed toward the purposeful adaption to and the selection and shaping of real world environments relevant to one's life, (2) the experiential sub-theory that proposes that performance on any task is an indication of intelligence only to the extent that it requires the ability to deal with novel tasks and/or the ability to automatize the processing of information and (3) the componential sub-theory in which the mechanism of information processing is specified: meta-components are executive processes used to plan, monitor and evaluate one's strategy for solving problems; and performance components are used to carry out the instructions of the meta-components for solving problems; and knowledge acquisition components are used to learn how to solve the problems in the first place.

Borkowski et al. (1987) elaborated a general model of intelligence that distinguished between: (1) the architectural system in intelligence; that is, the biologically, genetically based properties necessary for processing information, such as memory span, retention of stimulus traces and speed of encoding and decoding information; (2) the executive system, that is, the environmentally learned components that guide problem-solving such as long-term knowledge and its retrieval. In common with Sternberg, he stressed the importance of meta-cognition in the development of successful learning and discussed three perspectives: metacognition as one component of general intelligence interacting with other components throughout life; metacognition as the process that promotes the generalization of thinking strategies; and metacognition as a possible link between intelligence, self-knowledge and regulation.

A further influence upon the development of TASC was the Social Learning Theory of Bandura, who assumed that learning involved a three-way relationship between the environment, personal factors and behavior (including cognitive behavior).

The relationship between each of these influences is bi-directional. For example, membership of differing social classes may activate differential social treatments, leading to varying influences upon self-concept, which in turn influence perception of events and consequent actions. Bandura refers to this as "reciprocal determinism".

There are three components of learning. First are the modeled behaviors, which may be live, verbal or symbolic. The characteristic of a model stimulus (observed behavior of parents, peers, teachers, recipes or instructions, television, film) is that it is so organized that the learner can extract and act upon information conveyed, without needing to act overtly. Second, there are the consequences of behavior, which might be direct reinforcement, vicarious reinforcement or vicarious punishment, or self-reinforcement whereby the learner has self-prescribed standards of behavior, has reinforcing events under his/her control and is able to act as his/her own reinforcing agent. Third, there are the learner's cognitive processes – his or her ability to encode and store transitory experiences in symbolic form and represent future consequences in thought. These cognitive processes include attention, retention, motor production and motivational processes.

The acquisition of complex skills and abilities depends upon two additional components. These are perceived self-efficacy, where learners believe they can successfully execute the behavior required to produce a particular outcome, and self-regulation, setting standards for one's own capability of self-observation, self-judgment and self-response. These make possible self-direction (goal-setting and self-evaluation).

Structure and Implementation of Thinking Actively in Social Contexts

The TASC wheel is the central device (see Figure 8.1), involving eight concepts: Gather/Organize (information and data), Identify (what is the problem?), Generate (think of as many ideas

FIGURE 8.1 The TASC Wheel

(Reproduced with permission from Belle Wallace.)

as possible), Decide (Which is the best one?), Implement (Do or Make), Evaluate (How well did we do? How can we do better?), Communicate (How can we share our ideas?), and Learn from Experience (Reflect on what have we learned).

Further details about four of these (Gather and Organize, Identify, Communicate, Reflect and Learn from Experience) are given below.

Gather and Organize: What do we already know? Gathering and Organizing Incoming Information involves giving attention to detail and being precise and accurate when necessary, considering more than one source of information simultaneously, giving names to objects, events, ideas, experiences, in order to aid memory and communication, developing spatial and temporal concepts and relationships, deciding which features of an object remain constant even when changes occur and recognizing, interpreting and being able to follow instructions.

Identify and Solve Problems involves relating new data to previous experiences, being aware of disequilibrium, incompletion and incongruity, distinguishing between relevant and irrelevant information, selecting of representation: for example, codes, conventions, symbols, diagrams, pictures, drawings, tables, charts, summaries, key words, spider diagrams; seeking relationships between objects, events, experiences, keeping in mind various pieces of information, comparing objects, events, experiences; finding the class or set to which objects, events, experiences belong; understanding and using spatial and temporal references and patterns, including various viewpoints, analyzing information, problems into parts, synthesizing ideas from various sources, thinking about different possibilities; and consequences and using logical evidence to prove things and defend opinions.

Communicating with Co-learners and Communicating the Outcome involves avoiding egocentric communication; thinking things through before beginning to communicate; being clear and precise; avoiding blocking; selecting an appropriate mode for communication; giving instructions clearly; using logical evidence to defend opinions; being an active listener; comparing new experiences with previous ones; classifying objects, events, experiences, problems, solutions; considering other circumstances in which the information, experience, outcome, insight might apply; deriving rules and principles from experiences and hypothesizing; and predicting about related problems/issues.

Learning from experience involves comparing new experiences with previous ones, classifying objects, events, experiences, problems and solutions, considering other circumstances in which the information/experience/outcome/insight might apply, deriving rules and principles from experiences and hypothesizing and predicting about related problems/issues.

Skills and Processes

These involve giving attention to detail and being precise and accurate when necessary, considering more than one source of information simultaneously; and giving names to objects, events, ideas, experiences in order to aid memory and communication; developing spatial and temporal concepts and relationships; deciding which features of an object remain constant, even when changes occur; recognizing, interpreting and being able to follow instructions; using information to identify and solve problems; relating new data to previous experiences; being aware of disequilibrium/incompletion/incongruity; distinguishing between relevant and irrelevant information; selecting codes, conventions, symbols, diagrams. pictures, drawings, tables, charts, summaries, keywords, spider diagrams; seeking relationships between objects/events/experiences; keeping in mind various pieces of information; comparing objects/events/experiences; finding the class or set to which objects/events/experiences belong; understanding and using spatial/temporal references and patterns, including various viewpoints; analyzing information/problems into parts; synthesizing ideas from various sources; thinking about different possibilities and consequences and using logical evidence to prove things and defend opinions.

Tools for Thinking

The Thinking Tools involve systematically exploring and questioning available data using all the senses, which requires the ability to recognize that a problem exists in the first place.

Identifying requires the student to search for and explore further information, making comparisons with previous experiences, establishing the additional information that is needed, analyzing the problem into parts and establishing goals, selecting and organizing relevant information. Information gathered must be checked and represented in a form that is clear to the learner.

The Thinking Tools require the pupil to produce ideas, possibly by brainstorming, to research for further information, to consult with other people, to analyze previously used options and to hypothesize. They include looking at immediate, mid- and long-term consequences, consulting other people about their opinions and wishes, establishing priorities in order to select a course of action, making a case for the course of action chosen and planning a starting point, with sequences of working and ways of recording and monitoring. Students are required to constantly monitor progress and consider alternatives, if necessary, establish the criteria necessary for such checking, prepare alternative courses of action, continually check efficiency against previously made decisions and revise procedures if necessary.

Regarding evaluation, not only is assessing the solution necessary, but also the process of arriving at the solution, assessing the effectiveness of the use of personal thinking skills and strategies selected, examining the quality and efficacy of group interaction, and, if necessary, revising the whole problem-solving procedure. In communication, the student is required to exchange ideas on the solution of the problem and the process of problem-solving, justify decisions taken by evaluating the evidence on which they were based, exchange ideas on the efficiency of group interaction and organization and recall and explain succinctly to others.

Concerning reflection, although throughout the problem-solving process students are encouraged to reflect on their thinking processes, the TASC model has a definitive stage for analyzing and reflecting on the whole process of problem-solving, comparing present performance with previous performances, analyzing one's personal strengths and weaknesses, revising the whole problem-solving procedure, the strategies used, the resources called upon, seeking to generalize what has been learned and to transfer what has been learned to other situations.

Basic Pedagogical Principles

These basic principles are universally applicable to all learners. Differences of culture and context can be accommodated within them, thus providing for particular differences and emphases. The basic underlying principles are as follows:

1. Adopt a model of the problem-solving process, and explicitly teach this. A problem situation is defined as one in which a person or persons have a goal or goals that cannot be achieved because of an obstacle or obstacles: that is, Problem = Objective + Obstacle. Within TASC, students are given training in the identification and formulation of problems relevant to themselves. The model of the problem-solving process adopted is intended only as a starting point and certainly should not be regarded as the only possible one.

2. Identify a set of specific skills and strategies, and give training in these. As with the training of any skill, one can lay down a sequence of events, namely: demonstrate, analyze and label sub-skills, practice sub-skills and improve these by means of external feedback, build the sub-skills into complex skills and improve these to the point of automatization of use. This has implications for the manner in which the sub-skills and complex skills are dealt with in any thinking skills training course. It does, however, beg the issue of which skills are to be trained. Here, TASC has taken a pragmatic approach, whereby a set of skills relevant to the successive stages of the problem-solving model were selected (goal-setting, prioritization, brainstorming, weighing evidence, considering varying viewpoints and so forth). The list of skills became gradually more specific and revealed the need for more basic functions, such as comparisons, analogies, and for more complex strategies such as working backward from a goal, or means-end analysis.

3. Develop a vocabulary, including verbal labels and visual mnemonics suited to the age and social background of the students. For example, "evaluate" may be replaced by

questions such as "Have we solved the problem?" "How well did our solution work?" This negotiated vocabulary is essential if students are to engage in reflection on their own performance and discussion of their own thought processes in order to internalize the problem-solving process and the thinking skills.

4. Give ample practice in both the skills and the strategies, using situations that are significant and relevant to the learners. Wherever possible, the learners' own problems should form the basis of their learning. Their own experiences should be the starting points for their analysis and the development of more effective cognitive functioning.

5. Give attention to the motivational aspects of problem-solving. Many disadvantaged youngsters turn away from tackling problems out of a sense of learned helplessness. They perceive themselves as "incapable", as victims in a world where others are powerful and they are powerless. The course must help to build a positive self-concept and attempt to move the learner toward an internal locus of control. The children need to learn how to resolve conflict between the old and the new, the dominant value systems and the less dominant value systems. It is therefore essential to ensure early successes, and to provide constant positive reinforcement to "empower" students by giving them experiences by which they can identify themselves as successful problem-solvers.

6. The progression of teaching is from modeling by teacher, to guided activity by the learner and eventually autonomous action by the learner. The teacher must be sensitive to the rate of learning and development of confidence of the learner, gradually removing his/her intervention (scaffolding) as the student gains mastery.

7. Every effort must be made to enable the learner to transfer skills and strategies learned in the course to new contexts. This will involve employing any given skill in as wide a range of contexts as possible and in getting pupils to explicitly identify links with the school syllabuses and with out-of-school contexts.

8. The emphasis is upon co-operative learning in small groups. This enhances the opportunities for participation by each individual. The emphasis is also upon oral communication, which encourages confidence and develops language and thinking skills.
9. The teachers should encourage pupils' self-monitoring and self-evaluation, and the ability to learn from errors and partial failures as well as successes. Feedback from the teacher is essential and pupils should be guided not only in the assessment of the end result of the problem-solving process but also on the problem-solving process itself.
10. Throughout activities, students will be required to develop their metacognitive knowledge, that is, information about their own cognitive as well as their metacognitive skills. Constant introspection and guided reflection by the learner, and the verbalization of his/her personal progress and insights, are essential if the learner is to become increasingly aware of his/her thinking processes.

Examples of Thinking Actively in Social Contexts Activities

One specific activity in a course for secondary students aged 14 focused on pupils' capacities to analyze, organize and reproduce a complex geometric figure before and after mediation. The complex figures A and B (Figures 8.2 and 8.3) each consist of a geometric line-drawing with internal and external detail consisting of 18 elements.

Complex figure A was displayed and subjects were asked to "make the best copy you can". During copying, subjects were instructed at the end of every two-minute period to change the color of pen used. This indicated the sequence in which elements of the figure were drawn and hence revealed the strategy the subject had adopted. No time limit was imposed, although after ten minutes subjects were asked if they needed more time: if so. this was allowed. A range of strategies emerged. Some subjects made totally unplanned, unsystematic attempts. Others used a

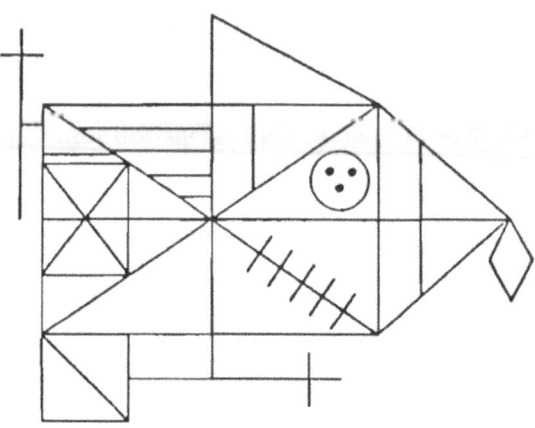

Complex Figure A

FIGURE 8.2 Complex Figure Drawing A
(Reproduced with permission from Belle Wallace.)

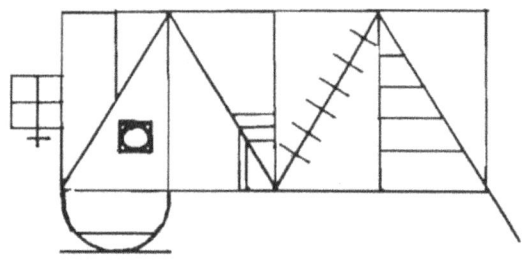

Complex Figure B

FIGURE 8.3 Complex Figure Drawing B
(Reproduced with permission from Belle Wallace.)

discernible strategy which was more or less effective. Such strategies included starting with a general outline which included parts of the central rectangle plus appendages without any attempt to differentiate; using the central point of the rectangle as a datum; using another point (such as top left-hand corner) as a datum; taking a major element (such as the large rectangle) and subdividing this both internally and externally.

After the initial copying (task 1) the poster was removed, and there was a two-minute period of unrelated activity. Subjects were then asked to reproduce the figure from memory (task 2), again changing pen color at the end of each two-minute interval. Not surprisingly, in every case the strategy adopted in task 1 was also adopted in task 2, although the degree of congruence between individual subjects' scores on task 1 and task 2 varied greatly. At this point the subjects as a group were given a session of strategy training. It was stressed that there was no one correct method of achieving a perfect reproduction of the figure and that the emphasis was upon "thinking about how we think".

Instruction focused on:

- Avoiding impulsive action (think first, act later).
- The necessity of defining problem situations (What is the goal? What are the obstacles within the problem field or within the problem-solver?)
- The necessity of exploring a situation fully, giving attention to detail and being precise about gathering, recording and remembering information.
- Using verbal labels (rectangle, diagonal, quarter, inside/outside) and making analogies for the whole or parts of the figure (a house on its side, a spaceship, a fish's fin, a button, a face).
- Devising a strategy (planning, implementing it and monitoring progress) that was sensible and effective in the given circumstances. This includes being able to answer questions such as, Where do I start? What comes next? How do I check that I have done it correctly? Have I finished?

After the session of strategy training. subjects were again asked to copy complex figure A from the poster (task 3) and after a further intervening period of three minutes, to reproduce it again from memory (task 4). The changes in strategy as opposed to improvements merely in speed or accuracy of production were then used as an indication of a subject's cognitive modifiability. The group-training was felt to equate more closely to a school learning situation than would individual assessment, even though the latter might be assumed to be more effective.

An obvious criticism at this point is that improvement in performance on tasks 3 and 4, still using complex figure A, may be a result of practice (a so-called test effect). However, use of an alternative figure, complex figure B, indicated the impact of strategy training as opposed to mere practice. In an attempt to assess the durability of the improved performance, the copying task (task 5) using figure B was given three days after strategy training and reproduction from memory (task 6) followed task 5 with an intervening three hours of intellectually demanding but unrelated work. All subjects retained almost in entirety the individual changes achieved between tasks 1 and 2 and tasks 3 and 4 (that is, pre- and post-training).

Training for Thinking Actively in Social Contexts

TASC International is at https://www.tascwheel.co.uk and has a section headed Training. A training video is also available. The website includes Live Virtual Training by way of introduction, Recorded Virtual Training (a half-day program), a face-to-face Introduction including materials that can be a half-day or full day, Subject Specific training which relates TASC to curriculum subjects, and Advanced Training for the more experienced. The TASC wheel is available on the website in Latin American Spanish, Welsh, Portuguese, Italian, Hungarian, German, Gaelic, French, Danish, Dutch and European Spanish. A booklet entitled 101 TASC Ideas is also freely downloadable.

The TASC Framework was developed into a school series of language and thinking texts for pupils ranging from Year 1 to Year 12. Belle Wallace has written a series of problem-solving and thinking skills books (see the References and Bibliography). Materials have included: TASC Wheel classroom laminated poster (A0/A1 size), TASC Wheel classroom laminated poster (A2), 15 wipe-clean laminated reusable TASC boards for pupils, TASC A3 colored postcards for children to keep on their tables for quick reference, TASC DVD in which children explain how they have used TASC, a CD-ROM with examples of TASC lesson plans and a disposable 16-page TASC booklets for pupils to record their thinking (with simple instructions, full icon and TASC images and color-coded pages for each segment of the TASC Wheel).

Extensions of Thinking Actively in Social Contexts

Although originally developed in the very challenging context of the Zulu homeland, TASC has since been spread to the UK (including Welsh and Gaelic), Spain, Italy, Portugal, Germany, France, Denmark, Holland, Hungary, Latin America, Jordan, Indonesia and China. Although originally developed as a content-free method that could be applied independently or to any subject, more detailed advice about linking TASC to a whole variety of subjects is now available.

References and Bibliography

Adams, H. B., & Wallace, B. (1988). The assessment and development of potential of high school pupils in the third world context of KwaZuluINatal: (Part III) Developing higher order thinking skills and problem-solving strategies in a cooperative learning environment. *Gifted Education International*, *5*(3), https://doi.org/10.1177/026142948800500302

Awwad, F. M. A., Asha, I. K., & Jado, S. M. A. (2014). The effect of TASC wheel on developing self-directed learning readiness and academic self-efficacy on a sample of 7th graders in Jordan. *Education*, *135*(2), 237–251. ERIC Number: EJ1095387

Borkowski, J. G., Carr, M., & Pressley, M. (1987). "Spontaneous" strategy use: Perspectives from metacognitive theory. *Intelligence*, *11*(1), 61–75. https://doi.org/10.1016/0160-2896(87)90027-4

Fauziah, M., Marmoah, S., Murwaningsih, T., & Saddhono, K. (2020). The effect of thinking actively in a social context and creative problem-solving learning models on divergent-thinking skills viewed from adversity quotient. *European Journal of Educational Research*, *9*(2), 537–568. https://doi.org/10.12973/eu-jer.9.2.537

Mounter, J., Huxtable, M., & Whitehead, J. (2019). Using thinking actively in a social context and spirals in living theory research in explanations of educational influences in a global social movement. *Gifted Education International*, *35*(2), 91–109. https://doi.org/10.1177/0261429418824110

Susanto, R., & Suryadarma, I. G. P. (2019). Thinking actively in social contexts for improving creative thinking skills. *Psychology, Evaluation, and Technology in Educational Research*, *2*(1), 51–62. https://doi.org/10.33292/petier.v2i1.14

Wallace, B. (1983). *Teaching the very able child*. London: Ward Lock.

Wallace, B. (2001). *Teaching thinking skills across the primary curriculum*. London: David Fulton Publishers.

Wallace, B. (2002a). *Teaching thinking skills across the early years*. London: David Fulton Publishers.

Wallace, B. (2002b). *Teaching thinking skills across the middle years*. London: David Fulton Publishers.

Wallace, B. (2003). *Using history to develop thinking skills at Key Stage 2*. London: David Fulton Publishers.

Wallace, B., Cave, D., & Berry, A. (2008). *Teaching problem-solving and thinking skills through science*. London: Routledge.

Wallace, B., Bernardelli, A., Molyneux, C., & Farrell, C. (2012). TASC: Thinking actively in a social context. A universal problem-solving process: A powerful tool to promote differentiated learning experiences. *Gifted Education International*, *28*(1), 58–83. doi: https://doi.org/10.1177/0261429411427645

Wallace, B., Humphries, W., & Evans, K. (2019). On demonstrating the development of the Thinking Actively in a Social Context (TASC) problem-solving approach in schools in South Wales (UK). *Gifted Education International*, *35*(2), 152–160. https://doi.org/10.1177/0261429419839380

Wallace, B., Maker, J., Cave, D., & Chandler, S. (2004). *Thinking skills and problem-solving: An inclusive approach*. London: David Fulton Publishers.

Wardhani, I. Y. (2018). Learning to think actively in social context to improve capabilities of higher order thinking in high school students. *Journal of Biology Education*, *1*(1), http://journal.stainkudus.ac.id/index.php/jbe

Section C

Programs Outside the Traditional Curriculum

Some programs are typically taught outside the traditional curriculum, although they may relate to it. Obviously, this means that teachers must renounce some part of the traditional curriculum in order to make the space and time to teach them, and this decision is often difficult. Alternatively, the programs can be taught in school but outside the traditional curriculum, as a lunchtime or after-school club, but then obviously will reach only the students who are committed to participating.

9

Instrumental Enrichment (IE)

Instrumental Enrichment is a program for helping people improve their intellectual performance by developing the cognitive skills relevant to the successful performance of intellectual tasks. First used for students/pupils with intellectual disabilities, Instrumental Enrichment was later applied to all ages and intellectual levels. The program involves solving puzzles, some of which are similar to the kinds of problems found in conventional intelligence tests, as well as bridging, which involves relating performance on these puzzles to the solution of real-world problems. IE is a context-free cognitive intervention program – it focuses on cognitive processes, not on any specific content. It is deliberately advocated that the program be taught outside the traditional classroom, where initial "bad habits" of thinking may be practiced.

IE was formulated in the 1970s by Romanian-born Israeli psychologist Reuven Feuerstein (1921–2014), known for his theory of intelligence, which stated it was not fixed, but rather modifiable. Feuerstein's 1980 book *Instrumental Enrichment* is a classic. Feuerstein was the founder and director of the International Center for the Enhancement of Learning Potential (ICELP) in Jerusalem. For more than 50 years, Feuerstein's theories and applied systems have been implemented in both clinical and classroom settings internationally, with more than 80 countries applying his work.

Effects of Instrumental Enrichment

The first evaluation study of a two-year IE program was reported by Feuerstein in the 1980 book. It involved a matched pairs experiment involving 114 low achieving pupils (average IQ = 80) from culturally and economically deprived backgrounds, aged 12–15. Intensive preliminary and ongoing training was provided for the teachers involved. Despite a previous dismissal of conventional IQ tests, the main measure was the Thurstone Scale of Primary Mental Abilities – a conventional group IQ test. The experimental group showed statistically significant improvement over the control group on the average overall PMA score and four of the eight subtests. Out of 12 attainment tests, statistically significant improvement was shown on only two – Bible studies and geometry.

A number of implementation problems were identified. Qualitative evaluation of implementation was by means of weekly and monthly teacher reports, daily annotated logs of teachers and observers, transcripts of staff meetings and questionnaires and interviews with students and teachers. From an initial position of ambivalence from both teachers and students, shifts in attitude were reported over the two years. Finally, all teachers reported great satisfaction in their work, expressed a willingness to continue teaching IE and felt that their students had benefited from the program. They reported increased student motivation, alertness and intellectual curiosity, a readiness to work independently and an increased sense of personal responsibility.

In relation to long-term follow-up, the Israeli research team reassessed a comparatively large number of their former subjects two years after the completion of IE training on their entry into the army. Ninety-seven IE trained subjects and 90 original controls were administered an intelligence test, and highly significant differences were found in favor of the IE group, displaying cumulative gains over time, in contrast with the reported long-term effects of most intervention studies.

Beyond this, research on the efficacy of IE has been conducted with several varied populations, including engineers at a Motorola plant in the USA, impoverished students in rural communities in Bahia Brazil, deaf non-literate immigrants from Ethiopia (Lurie & Kozulin, 1995), autistic and Down Syndrome children in Jerusalem, low-performing high school mathematics students and weak middle grade readers in the USA and many other groups. However, many of these reports are difficult to track down and many are brief descriptions rather than evaluations.

Savell et al. (1986) examined some 35 reports of IE interventions. Studies finding statistically significant effects usually provided subjects with a greater dosage (in the form of instruments and classroom hours) of IE than studies that did not. Some form of training for instructors was necessary if IE was to be effective, but the amount of this was more difficult to quantify. Likewise, some minimum number of hours of student exposure to IE was likely necessary. The studies reviewed suggested that at least a week of IE training for instructors was needed prior to the first year of teaching, plus follow-up support during that year and additional training prior to the second year. Generally, 80 hours or more of student exposure to IE over a one- or two-year period was necessary for effectiveness. The effects observed were on standard nonverbal measures of intelligence (e.g., Lorge-Thorndike, Cattell and Ravens) – tests that were largely measures of skill in processing figural and spatial information. A number of other measures had been included (e.g., measures of self-concept, classroom behavior, impulsivity, academic achievement and course content), but effects were absent, inconsistent, or difficult to interpret.

In the same year, Sternberg and Bhana (1986) produced a review of intellectual skills programs with the striking sub-title "Snake-Oil Remedies or Miracle Cures?" This reviewed 38 studies of IE, from many different populations in many different countries. Variable dosage was noted, with greater dosage generally leading to larger gains. When fully and properly implemented, gains were achievable on IQ type tests (largest in abstract reasoning and spatial visualization) and aptitude measures. There was some evidence of transfer to school subjects, but this depended on the skill of the individual teacher in "bridging".

In 1987, Shayer and Beasley also reviewed IE studies, coming to essentially the same conclusion. Their additional small-scale empirical study yielded effect sizes of 1.22, 1.07 and 0.76. However, they pointed out that all evaluations to that point had been done at the end of the intervention period (although this could be as long as three years) and there was a scarcity of subsequent follow-up measures.

Romney and Samuels (2001) noted that some proponents of IE claimed an improvement in cognitive ability, school achievement and classroom behavior. They conducted a meta-analysis of a total of 40 controlled studies. Significant, though modest, average effect sizes were found in all three areas – achievement, ability and behavior – with the most extensive improvement being made in ability. Gains in spatial/perceptual ability were related to the length of the intervention (number of hours). Self-esteem was related to age, with older children showing increases and young children showing decreases.

In a spin-off from IE, Blagg (1991) developed a form of it which could be delivered by ordinary schoolteachers in regular lessons. The Somerset Thinking Skills Course is a set of materials consisting of a handbook and seven modules: foundations of problem-solving, analyzing and synthesizing, positions in space and time, predicting and deciding and so on. The materials are all pictorial and naturalistic rather than content-free as in IE. The principles of mediation, bridging and transfer remained relevant. The program was taught for two to two-and-a-half hours per week to an average total of 112 hours. In a two-year evaluation in four schools, Blagg found no significant improvements in intervention groups compared to controls on intellectual performance or tests of reading and mathematics skills. These disappointing results were attributed to weaknesses in the training. However, the teachers who used IE became more assertive, confident and self-reliant, and also more satisfied with their jobs, more committed to their profession and more valued in their work. Thus, the program might have done more for the teachers than it did for the students.

In a doctoral thesis, Shiell (2002) meta-analyzed 36 studies from 1979 to 1996. There were effect sizes of 0.24 for non-verbal ability, 1.41 for verbal ability, and 0.60 for full-scale ability. Effect sizes for visual perception and visual-motor ability were 0.42, 0.71 and 1.68. Effect sizes for general achievement and math achievement were 0.26 and 0.29, respectively. The locus of control effect size was 0.33, but effect sizes for reading and the Learning Potential Assessment Device (LPAD) were small.

Other more recent studies have reported only single empirical ventures. Significant among these were Kozulin et al. (2010), who investigated the then-new "Instrumental Enrichment Basic" program (IE-basic), aimed at systematic perception, self-regulation abilities, conceptual vocabulary, planning, decoding emotions and social relations. Participants were children with various problems from Canada, Chile, Belgium, Italy and Israel. Experimental children ($N = 104$) received only 27–90 hours of the program during 30–45 weeks, while the comparison groups ($N = 72$) received general occupational and sensory-motor therapy. Pre-post gain scores showed a statistically significant advantage of the experimental over comparison group in three WISC-R subtests (Similarities, Picture Completion, Picture Arrangement) and Raven's Matrices. Effect sizes ranged from 0.30 to 0.52.

In 2011, Tzuriel sought to show the utility of dynamic assessment (DA) in three programs: IE, Bright Start and Peer Mediation with Young Children. In all three programs, DA was more effective than standardized tests in revealing effects. However, in several previous studies, the LAPD did not distinguish between intervention and non-intervention groups. In 2023, Tzuriel et al. reported an empirical study of IE for one year in three Grade 4 classes ($n = 73$) in an Israeli-Arab school for girls, with two control classes ($n = 58$). Measures were grades in English, Arabic and mathematics. IE students significantly improved their grades compared with controls and lower cognitive students benefited more than higher students. Thus, later studies have shown effects from shorter periods of IE that generalized to academic achievement. Other later studies have found effects of IE on reading comprehension, physical education, self-control and internal locus of control and science achievement.

Theoretical Underpinnings of Instrumental Enrichment

The idea of "mediated learning" is central to Feuerstein's theory of cognitive development. Cognitive mediation means that some external agent (usually but not always an adult) intentionally demonstrates to a learner a method to interpret information or solve problems, for example, the usefulness of categorization as a method for interpretation, with a view to the learner subsequently being able to perform that or a similar task with support or scaffolding from the adult, leading to the learner being able to perform the task unaided, leading to the leaner being able to bridge or transfer the technique to other problems for which this might be a solution.

Mediated learning experience (MLE) refers to the way in which stimuli emitted by the environment are transformed by a "mediating" agent, usually a parent, sibling, peer or other caregiver. This mediating agent selects and organizes the world of stimuli for the child. The mediator selects stimuli that are most appropriate and then frames, filters and schedules them; s/he determines the appearance or disappearance of certain stimuli. The child acquires behavior patterns and learning sets, which in turn become important ingredients of his capacity to become modified through direct exposure to stimuli.

Intentionality and reciprocity are key conditions for achieving mediated learning experience. The mediator implements intentionality when guiding interaction toward a goal, selecting, organizing and interpreting certain stimuli. Reciprocity is checked when there is a good response from the subject and it is demonstrated that s/he is responsive and involved in the learning process. Reciprocity is a key issue because the child realizes that its actions can be decisive in action with the world. The three elements influencing and involved in intentionality and reciprocity are: (1) the mediator – whose language, rhythm, tone of voice and body language can be exploited to increase the intentionality, (2) the mediated person – whose attention, interest level and availability influence reciprocity, (3) the stimulus – (presentation of ideas and material), which may show variations in terms of amplitude, repeated presentation and exposure method, to facilitate both intentionality and reciprocity.

Mediation of meaning occurs when the mediator communicates with the other person the meaning and purpose of an activity. Meaning is mediated by assigning signification, both at the cognitive/intellectual and affective/emotional levels. Values and beliefs are communicated at the cognitive level; energy and enthusiasm are communicated at the emotional level. Mediation of transcendence occurs when the mediator acts so that the mediated learning experience emerges from the context in which it occurred and goes beyond its limits, expanding and diversifying the needs of the mediated person. Its purpose is to promote acquisition of principles, concepts and strategies that can be generalized and used in new or similar situations; This involves: (1) association of present events with events from the past or with future events, (2) engaging in reflective thinking to reach deep understanding of the situation and (3) collateral thinking on experience and problems.

Another key element is the Learning Potential Assessment Device (LPAD), which offers an alternative to traditional psychometric assessments. The LPAD focuses on the individuals' learning potential rather than on their manifest level of performance. The application of LPAD allows for setting up higher educational, social and vocational goals for disabled individuals and prevents their labeling as uneducable or unsuitable for intervention. The LPAD helps to identify culturally different children whose true learning potential is obscured by the lack of familiarity with a new culture. These children are expected to respond positively to mediation provided during the assessment (the term "dynamic assessment" has the same connotation). If the difference between their pre- and post-mediation scores is substantial, they are likely to benefit from IE.

Cognitive deficit is seen as blurred or sweeping perceptions of the environment, impulsivity, inability to select the cues that are relevant to defining problems, many trial-and-error responses, imprecision in communicating information, and so on. IE aims to correct students' deficient cognitive functions – unsystematic exploratory behavior, lack of planning, absence of the need for logical evidence, egocentric nature of responses and so forth.

Structure and Implementation of Instrumental Enrichment

The IE standard program goal is to correct deficiencies in fundamental thinking skills, and to provide students with the concepts, skills, strategies, operations and techniques necessary to function as independent learners. Deliberately free of specific subject matter, the tasks in the "instruments" are intended to be transferable (bridged) to all educational and everyday life situations. In 2000, Feuerstein added IE-BASIC to prevent learning problems in younger children (3 to 8 years old) and to help low performing older children.

The program itself consists of more than 500 pages of paper-and-pencil exercises, divided into 14 different instruments. The instruments themselves are broken down into carefully selected series of small steps designed to lead the participant from a simple introductory level to complex higher-order thinking. Thus, there is progression over the two to three years of one-hour lessons (i.e., 400 to 500 hours) that constitute the full program.

The early instruments cover pattern detection, pattern comparisons and orientation in space. The later instruments move on to more complex reasoning and problem solving (e.g., syllogisms, transitive relations, representations). The teacher's role is critical to help explore problem definitions, encourage evaluation of strategies, an help to develop language to describe and discuss thought processes, as well as engaging in bridging exercises to encourage transfer to the mainstream curriculum.

Instrumental Enrichment Basic is aimed at younger children (aged 5–7) and older children with serious cognitive deficiencies, covering: (1) perceptual–motor development, oriented toward visuo-motor coordination, attention and planning behavior (Organization of Dots-B, Tri-Channel Attentional Learning, Spatial Orientation, Orientation in Space-B); (2) decoding emotional expression and understanding their social/behavioral correlates (Identifying Emotions; From Empathy to Action);

(3) abstractive/integrative thinking (From Unit to Group; Knowledge; Compare and Discover the Absurd; Thinking to Learn to Prevent Violence; Learning to Question for Reading Comprehension).

From Unit to Group helps children to establish the concept of number and basic mathematical operations by discovering the way in which objects can be aggregated, segregated, summarized and described. The tasks include counting and grouping simple visual stimuli such as dots, triangles, circles, squares and the like. The instrument promotes systematic exploration of data, systematic following of rules and consideration of several sources of information, comparison, categorization, inferential thinking and deductive reasoning. Orientation in Space-Basic is aimed at developing spatial concepts and orientation in two-dimensional pictorial space representing everyday life situations. This requires scanning the pictorial information, identifying the relative position of objects and events and the development of a conceptual vocabulary. The tasks include responding to verbal instructions.

Identifying Emotions develops the children's ability to decode behavioral and social cues that signify emotional states. At the top of each page there is a stimulus photograph showing certain emotional states and four pictures showing different life situations. Children are first mediated to look at the top photograph and label the emotion, and then to analyze each one of the "stories" depicted in four illustrations in terms of relevant emotional states of the characters involved. Compare and Discover the Absurd uses absurd or incongruous situations in a cartoon modality in order to develop the children's ability to use selected criteria as a basis for comparison and to develop a system of sub- and super-ordinate concepts. Both more basic (size, shape, direction, quantity) as well as more complex (age, function) criteria are used. The instrument is aimed at developing higher cognitive functions, expressive language and coordination of pictorial analysis with verbal responses.

However, IE may have some possible weaknesses. It requires very extensive teacher training if it is to be effective. Additionally, transfer to the traditional curriculum may be aimed for, but may not happen. Feuerstein emphasized that a great deal of time should be spent bridging, but it is possible that this area is neglected by extremely busy teachers.

Examples of Instrumental Enrichment Activities

Examples of the kind of materials in the IE program include: (a) orientation of dots, requiring students to identify and outline geometric figures within relatively amorphous arrays of dots, (b) comparisons, requiring students to point out how two similar-looking objects differ from each other, (c) categorization, requiring students to figure out to which of several categories pictures of common objects belong, (d) temporal relations, requiring students to indicate whether a given period of time is greater than, equal to, or less than another period of time and (e) numerical progressions, requiring students to generate continuations of a series of numbers.

In the Organization of Dots instrument, the child must identify and draw figures in an unorganized cloud of dots. The required figures are projected on an unformulated and unintelligible group of dots, which allows for several possibilities of projections. To reveal the figure, the child must overcome the complexity of the display and employ a well-planned and methodical strategy. This instrument is aimed at developing children's figural and visual–motor capabilities. The child identifies a geometric shape presented as a model in an amorphous cloud of dots. The child learns to overcome difficulties caused by the rotation of the figures and the proximity of the dots. The instrument promotes analytic perception of shapes, conservation of form and size, planning, need for precision and restraint of impulsivity.

In the Illustrations instrument, students are introduced to tasks aimed at producing an awareness of the existence of a problem, thus leading to disruption of equilibrium, cognitive incongruence and search for a solution. Each task is composed of a set of pictures portraying a problem (or an absurdity). The solution for the problem may depend on decoding of details and connecting them to previous familiar experiences. An example would be a sequence of pictures with a story behind them. For example, a mouse notices a lump of cheese lying on a high table that cannot be reached. To obtain the cheese, the mouse digs a hole starting at one foot of the table. As a result, the table is tilted to one side and the lump of cheese falls so that the mouse can eat it. Children are asked to explain the portrayed sequence and bridge it to other familiar situations. In Comparison instruments, students are required to compare sets of objects or events (for both differences and commonalities) along several dimensions (e.g., size, number, color, position, darkness).

However, finding specific examples is quite difficult given the tight control exerted by the originators of the program. Nonetheless, the following can be given courtesy of David Tzuriel (Figures 9.1 and 9.2).

Training for Instrumental Enrichment

Some users of IE are critical of the tight control of IE materials and extensive training required of teachers. The materials are available only to those trained in their use and trained teachers can only train other teachers if they have been trained as trainers and so on. The originators of the materials vigorously resist any form of adaptation or change in the instruments. However, given the research evidence on the relationship between thorough training and effectiveness and the disappointing findings of Blagg (1991) when he tried a user-friendly modified version, one can quite see the point of this.

The dissemination of the MLE, LPAD and IE programs is achieved through the network of Authorized Training Centers. These centers currently function in 40 countries. The Feuerstein Institute (https://www.icelp.info/centers) has a list of approved courses. Accredited IE training is available in the UK from the Binoh Centre in London (now known as Norwood – https://norwood.org.uk). Awareness days and two-thirds-day interactive workshops for the Somerset Thinking Skills Course are available from Nigel Blagg Associates (see Publications at http://www.nigelblaggassociates.co.uk).

134 ◆ Programs Outside the Traditional Curriculum

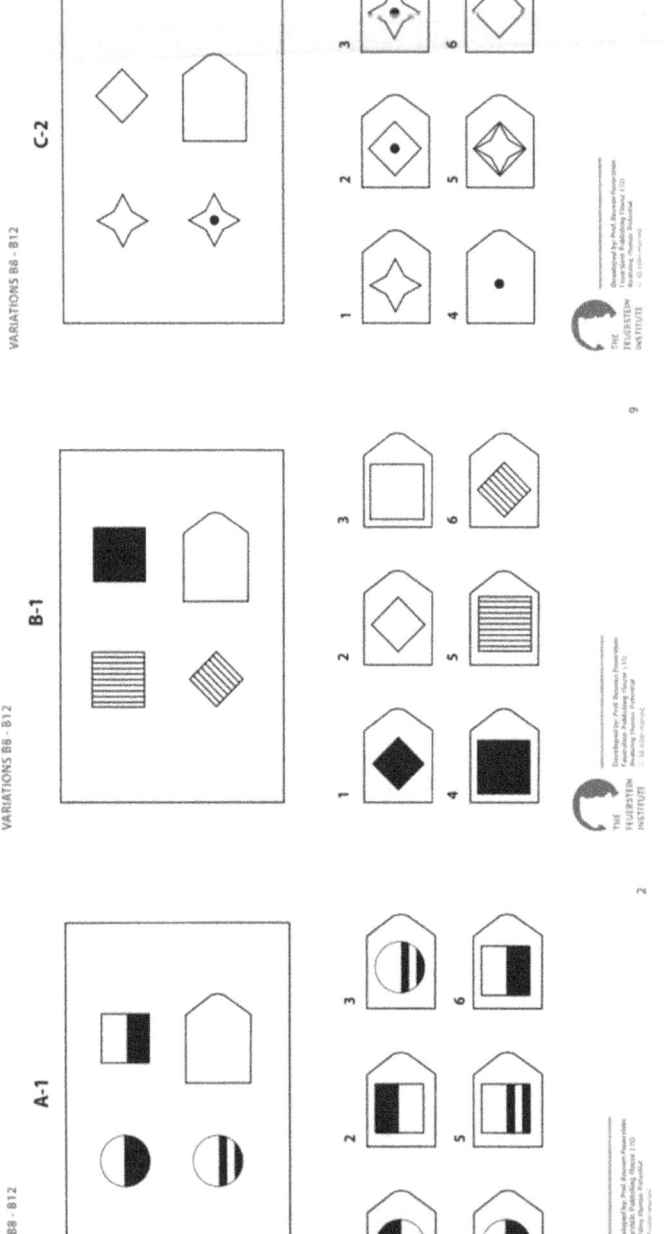

FIGURE 9.1 Examples of problems from B8 to B12 Variations test (reproduced with permission from David Tzuriel)

Problem									
5	2	5	8	11	14	17	20	___	___
9	5	8	7	8	9	8	11	___	___

FIGURE 9.2 Examples of problems from the Numerical Progression test of the LPAD (reproduced with permission from David Tzuriel)

Extensions of Instrumental Enrichment

IE currently operates in 80 countries. The Instrumental Enrichment materials have been translated into a great number of languages, including English, French, German, Spanish, Basque, Catalan, Portuguese, Italian, Romanian, Hungarian, Czech, Flemish, Finnish, Arabic, Chinese, Korean and Japanese. A large IE program for public school students has been undertaken in the state of Bahia, Brazil. The program started in 1999 in 18 schools for 15,580 students. The plan was for more than 300,000 students in 270 schools to receive IE lessons from more than 6,000 teachers trained for this purpose. The student population of public schools in Bahia is characterized by a low socioeconomic status and a high percentage of students of African-Brazilian ancestry.

Similarly, IE has spread from elementary and secondary schools into universities and colleges and prominently into the workplace, with managers seeing it as a way of increasing flexibility and therefore productivity. Nigel Blagg also has a system for working with adults in the workplace. However, apart from Blagg, IE continues to insist upon full training.

References and Bibliography

Blagg, N. (1991). *Can we teach intelligence?* Hillsdale, NJ: Lawrence Erlbaum Associates.

Feuerstein, R. (1980). *Instrumental Enrichment: An intervention program for cognitive modifiability*. Baltimore: University Park Press.

Kozulin, A., Lebeer, J., Madella-Noja, A., Gonzalez, F., Jeffrey, I., Rosenthal, N., & Koslowsky, M. (2010). Cognitive modifiability of children with developmental disabilities: A multicentre study using Feuerstein's Instrumental Enrichment—Basic program. *Research in Developmental Disabilities*, https://doi.org/10.1016/j.ridd.2009.12.001

Lurie, L., & Kozulin, A. (1995). *Application of Instrumental Enrichment cognitive intervention program with deaf immigrant children from Ethiopia.* Paper presented at *the 18th International Congress on Education of the Deaf* (Tel Aviv, Israel, July 16–20, 1995). ERIC ED 391265.

Romney, D. M., & Samuels, M. T. (2001). A meta-analytic evaluation of Feuerstein's Instrumental Enrichment program. *Educational and Child Psychology*, *18*, 19–34.

Savell, J. M., Twohig, P. T., & Rachford, D. L. (1986). Empirical status of Feuerstein's "Instrumental Enrichment" (FIE) as a method of teaching thinking skills. *Review of Educational Research*, *56*(4), 381–409. https://doi.org/10.3102/00346543056004381

Shayer, M., & Beasley, F. (1987). Does instrumental enrichment work? *British Educational Research Journal*, *13*(2), 101–119. https://doi.org/10.1080/0141192870130201

Shiell, J. L. (2002). *A meta-analysis of Feuerstein's Instrumental Enrichment.* Unpublished PhD thesis, University of British Columbia. https://open.library.ubc.ca/soa/cIRcle/collections/ubctheses/831/items/1.0055041

Sternberg, R. J., & Bhana, K. (1986). Synthesis of research on the effectiveness of intellectual skills programs: Snake-oil remedies or miracle cures? *Educational Leadership*, *44*(2), 60–67.

Tzuriel, D. (2011). Revealing the effects of cognitive education programmes through dynamic assessment. *Assessment in Education: Principles, Policy & Practice*, *18*(2), 113–131. https://doi.org/10.1080/0969594X.2011.567110

Tzuriel, D., Cohen, S., Feuerstein, R., Devisheim, H., Zaguri-Vittenberg, S., Goldenberg, R., Yosef, L., & Cagan, A. (2023). Evaluation of the Feuerstein Instrumental Enrichment (FIE) program among Israeli-Arab students. *International Journal of School & Educational Psychology*, *11*(1), 95–110. https://doi.org/10.1080/21683603.2021.1951409

10
CoRT (Cognitive Research Trust)

CoRT (Cognitive Research Trust) is a package of 60 lessons in six levels for the teaching of constructive thinking in schools from the age of eight upwards. The CoRT Thinking Program includes generative and creative thinking as well as operational and constructive thinking. It is used by children and adults across a broad span of age and ability levels. The original CoRT program was associated with work on the Principles of Thinking, the Attention Tools, the Thinking Tools, a distinction between creative, critical and lateral thinking, the Six Thinking Hats and other developments.

CoRT was named after the Cognitive Research Trust, established by Dr. Edward de Bono (1933–2021) in Cambridge, England. De Bono was a Maltese physician, psychologist, author, inventor and broadcaster. He originated the term "lateral thinking", wrote 85 books with translations into 46 languages on thinking and was a proponent of the teaching of thinking as a subject in schools. Over 7 million students in over 30 countries (including the UK, the United States, Canada, Australia, Japan, Singapore, Venezuela and Ireland) have participated in his work. Perhaps unfortunately, de Bono's creative talent expressed itself in writing books and presenting about the method rather than evaluating it, and thorough evaluations are relatively scarce.

Effects of CoRT

Here we will concentrate on evaluations of schoolchildren, although there are also studies of university students and other groups. Curiously, there does not appear to be a systematic analysis or meta-analysis of CoRT. Nonetheless, de Bono does report that in an early study of 300 pupils, a large shift was found on the AH4 intelligence test. However, he argues that he did not expect CoRT training to have such results, since his program focuses on thinking in real-life situations. He says criterion-referenced performance tests that require pupils to apply their thinking skills to real-life situations with written or recorded output are much more appropriate, but of course are much more difficult to summarize. For de Bono, the widespread use of his tools is sufficient validation.

A study in 20 Cambridgeshire primary schools was conducted by Hunter-Grundin (1985) over two years. There were some differences between experimental and control classes in reading comprehension, arithmetic and logical reasoning (effect size of 0.17) in the second year, but not in the first year. Differences on tests of creativity were small and statistically significant for only 1 out of 12 tests in the first year and 3 out of 12 tests in the second year. However, the teacher training program had severe limitations, so implementation quality was an issue.

Edwards (1991) reviewed a number of evaluative studies and found many had methodological weaknesses. Edwards describes his own study, which had matched experimental and control groups on pre-, post- and four-week delayed tests. Only scores on the Thinking Approaches Questionnaire maintained significant gains at follow-up. However, there were significant gains in social sciences and languages, but not in science or mathematics. In a later study with Australian aboriginal children (Ritchie & Edwards, 1996) aiming to enhance creative thinking, it was found that the CoRT program could enhance creative thinking in mainstream classrooms, but not their scholastic aptitude, school achievement, thinking approaches, self-concept as a thinker and internal locus of control. Issues of implementation arose again.

More recent studies come from very various countries and are characterized by relatively small samples (and in some cases, very limited dosage and rather doubtful research design and operation). Rule and Barrera (2006) examined the role of CoRT in supporting problem-based learning in one third-grade class ($n = 21$) in a deprived rural neighborhood. The intervention was only five weeks long. Pre-post assessment of criterion-referenced science content, interest and vocabulary showed significant student gains. Students and teachers were enthusiastic and positive.

The influence of CoRT on creativity and particularly concept mapping performance was conducted by Kumari and Gupta (2014) with senior secondary school students (grades 9 and 10). Experimental and control groups ($n = 51$ in each) were selected by cluster random sampling. At post-test, the experimental group had significantly better concept map performance. Daher et al. (2017) used CoRT with grade 6 students ($n = 53$) divided into experimental and control groups, focusing on creative thinking. Experimental students significantly outperformed control students in creative thinking. Moreover, low ability students and high ability students significantly outperformed average students. There were no gender differences.

Critical thinking skills in talented students were the focus of research by Turkey (2019), who used the first and third levels of CoRT with 30 randomly selected male and female students compared to a control group of 30. The Watson Glaser critical thinking test showed a statistically significant effect in favor of the experimental group, with no gender effects. Mousa (2022) deployed CoRT with Iraqi English-language learners. Experimental students numbered 30, as did matched controls. The intervention period was only 12 weeks. There were significant differences between the experimental and control groups in favor of the experimental group. Zeyad and Hameed (2022) used CoRT4 twice per week over ten weeks with English as a Foreign Language fifth year preparatory school students in Iraq. There were 40 students in each of experimental and control groups. The experimental group improved on tests of recognition and production, but strangely no control results are given.

Overall, then, more recent studies have been more consistently positive about CoRT effects, particularly creative thinking, but some of the studies have been rather weak and there must be concerns about the quality of training and implementation integrity. Diligent searchers will undoubtedly find more similar studies. However, despite de Bono's resistance, research suggests CoRT does seem to have effects even when deployed for short periods.

Theoretical Underpinnings of CoRT

Much of the structure of CoRT came directly from the creative mind of de Bono. However, there are elements of underpinning theory. De Bono's book *Mechanisms of the Mind* (1969) suggests CoRT is based directly on a model of information handling called the self-organizing, self-stabilizing, active information net. That is, a central assumption underlying the program is that the mind is pattern making and pattern using. This model is not of itself very different from those proposed by other theoreticians, even though CoRT is. De Bono's model has been translated into a full computer simulation, but this is now difficult to trace.

Structure and Implementation of CoRT

The CoRT program is divided into six sections of ten lessons each. Each section covers one particular aspect of thinking. The sections are designed as coherent wholes, with one lesson adding to or qualifying aspects of the previous ones. Thus, when teachers use individual CoRT sections, they should use all the lessons in that section. The sections may be used in any order, but it is usually advisable to start with CoRT1. CoRT1 has been used as an abbreviated program of instruction in thinking skills in its own right. CoRT6 has also been used in this way, as have CoRT 1, 4 and 5 in combination. Here we will look in more detail at sections 1, 4 and 5.

CoRT1: Breadth
This section is concerned with helping students develop tools and habits for scanning widely around a thinking situation. The following tools are emphasized:

Treatment of Ideas (PMI): Deliberately examining ideas for good, bad and interesting points, instead of immediately rejecting them.
Rules: Draws together the first two lessons.
Consequences (C&S): Considering the immediate, short-term, medium-term and long-term consequences of alternative strategies.
Objectives (AGO): Selecting and defining objectives; being clear about one's aims and understanding those of others.
Planning: Draws together the two preceding lessons.
Priorities (FIP): Choosing from a number of different possibilities and alternatives: putting one's priorities in order.
Alternatives (APC): Generating new alternatives and choices, instead of feeling confined to the obvious ones.
Decisions: Draws together the two preceding lessons.
Viewpoint (OPV): Considering all the viewpoints involved in a situation.
Being Right 2: Knowing other ways of being right: (1) using names, labels and classifications and (2) making judgments.
Being Wrong 2: Knowing two ways of being wrong: (1) exaggerating, making unwarranted generalizations, and (2) basing conclusions on only part of the situation.
Outcome: Knowing what has been achieved at the end of an argument – distinguishing seven possible levels short of complete agreement.

CoRT4: Creativity
This section is concerned with creative thinking and includes elements of lateral thinking. The following tools are emphasized:

Yes, No and Po: Using ideas creatively while suspending judgment on their worth.
Stepping Stone: Using ideas, not for their own sake, but because they lead to other ideas.

Random Input: Entering random, unrelated ideas into a situation as a stimulus for new lines of thought.

Concept Challenge: Testing the uniqueness of concepts to identify other ways of doing things.

Dominant Idea: Identifying the dominant ideas in a situation, so that they can be pushed aside to allow other ideas to develop.

Define the Problem: Defining a problem exactly to make it easier to solve.

CoRT5: Information and Feeling

This section is concerned with the place of information and feeling in thinking. The following tools are emphasized:

Information (FI-FO): Knowing what information is available in thinking about a situation and what additional information is needed.

Remove the Faults: Assessing the faults associated with an idea in order to remove them.

Combination: Examining the attributes of seemingly unrelated ideas as an aid in creating new combinations of ideas.

Requirements: Using the requirements of a situation as a way of identifying new ways of coping with that situation.

Evaluation: Determining whether an idea fits the requirements of a situation and knowing its advantages and disadvantages.

Now we should familiarize ourselves further with some of the basic ideas.

Principles for Thinking

There are many important principles, but 12 is the maximum number that is practical.

1. Always be constructive.
    Too many people get into negative habits of thinking. They enjoy proving someone else to be wrong. They feel that it is enough to be critical.

There is a lack of the constructive and generative aspects of thinking.

There are times when it is necessary to be critical, but we need to esteem constructive thinking above critical thinking.

2. Think slowly and try to make things as simple as possible.

Except for a few emergency occasions there is no great merit in thinking quickly.

A great amount of thinking can be done in a short time even if you think slowly.

Always try to make things simple.

There is no merit in complication (except to impress others).

Is there a simpler way of looking at this?

3. Detach your ego from your thinking – stand back and look at your thinking.

The biggest obstacle to skilled thinking is ego involvement: "I must be right", "My idea must be best".

You need to be able to stand back and to look at what is going on in your thinking.

Just as you might be objective about your tennis skills, you should be able to be objective about your thinking.

4. At this moment, What am I trying to do? What is my focus and purpose?

Right now, what is the focus of my thinking?

What am I trying to achieve?

What tools or methods am I using?

Without this sense of focus and purpose, thinking is just a matter of drifting along from moment to moment, from point to point.

Effective thinking requires this sense of focus and purpose.

5. Be able to "switch gears". Know when to seek information, use logic and creativity.

In driving a car, you select the appropriate gear.

In playing golf you select the appropriate club.

In cooking you select the appropriate pan.

Creative thinking is different from logical thinking and from seeking information.

A skilled thinker must be skilled at all the different types of thinking.

It is not enough just to be creative or critical.

You need to know when and how to use the different types of thinking.

6. What is the outcome of my thinking – why do I believe that it will work?

    Unless you can spell out a clear outcome of your thinking, you have wasted your time.

    If you have a conclusion, a decision, a solution or a design, you should be able to explain why you think it will work.

    At this point, how you got to the conclusion does not matter.

    Explain to yourself – as you would to someone else – why you think the outcome is going to work.

    If the outcome is a definition of a sticking point, a new problem or a better view of the matter, you need to say what you are going to do next.

7. Feelings and emotions are important to thinking, but after exploration, not before.

    We are often told that feelings and emotions must be kept out of thinking.

    This may be true for mathematics and science, but where people are concerned, feelings and emotions are an important part of thinking.

    But they need to be used at the right place.

    If feelings are used at the beginning, perception is limited and choice of action may be inappropriate.

    When exploration takes place first and when the alternatives have been examined, it is the role of feelings and emotions to make the final choice.

8. Always try to look for alternatives, for new perceptions and for new ideas.

    At every moment a skilled thinker will be trying to find alternatives: explanations, interpretations, action possibilities, different approaches.

When someone claims that there are "only two alternatives", the skilled thinker immediately tries to find others.

When an explanation is given as the only possible explanation, the skilled thinker tries to think of other explanations.

It is the same with the search for new ideas and new perceptions.

Is this the only way of looking at things?

9. Be able to move back and forth between broad-level and detail-level thinking.

In order to carry out any idea we have to think in terms of actual details.

So, at the end we do have to be specific.

But the ability also to think at the broad level (concept, function, abstract level) is a key characteristic of a skilled thinker.

This is the way we generate alternatives.

This is the way we move from one idea to another.

This is the way we link up ideas.

What is the broad idea here?

How can we carry out that broad idea?

10. Is this a matter of "maybe" or "must be"? Logic is only as good as the perception and information on which it is based.

This is a key principle because it deals with truth and logic.

When something is claimed to be true the claim is that it "must be" so.

When it is claimed that a conclusion "must follow" from what has gone, before, there is also an insistence on "must be".

If we can challenge this and show that it is only a matter of "may be", this may still have value but not the dogmatic value of truth and logic.

Even when the logic is without error, the conclusion only fits the perception and information on which the logic is based.

So, we need to look at this base.

In games and in belief systems we set things up to be true so they are true within that context.

In ordinary life we need always to distinguish between "may be" and "must be".

We need also to check what is claimed.

11. Differing views may all be soundly based on differing perceptions.

    When there are opposing views, we tend to feel that only one of these can be right.

    If you believe that you are right, you set out to show that differing views must be wrong.

    But differing views may be just as "right".

    A differing view may be soundly and logically based on a perception that is different from yours.

    This perception may include different information, different experiences, different values and a different way of looking at the world.

    In settling arguments and disagreements we need to become aware of the differing perceptions on both sides.

    We need to lay these out alongside each other and to compare them.

12. All actions have consequences and impact values, people and the world.

    Not all thinking results in action.

    Even when thinking does result in action, this action may be confined to a specific context such as mathematics, a scientific experiment, a game that is being played.

    In general, thinking that results in an action plan, a problem solution, a design, a choice or a decision is going to be followed by action.

    That action has future consequences.

    That action has an impact on the world around.

    This world includes values and other people.

    Action does not take place in a vacuum.

    Other people and the environment are always affected by decisions and initiatives.

CoRT Attention and Thinking Tools

Patterns are really attention or thinking tools or frames, designed to lead attention in a different direction from the conventional. One major common fault in thinking for both children and adults is the habit of taking an initial stand on a subject and then using thinking purely to support that stand – in other words, doing things backward. The attention director PMI (Plus, Minus and Interesting) (see below) helps address this, by requiring the student to consider minus as well as plus factors and interesting factors that require further exploration. The tools all have some acronym. This acronym is important and is not just jargon – it is necessary in order to turn an attitude into a usable tool. It is important that the tools should be used explicitly, formally and deliberately. This can be done as a request or as an invitation: "I want you to do an OPV" or "first of all I am going to do an AGO".

PMI: Plus, Minus and Interesting

A simple, attention-directing scan.

Instead of just backing up our first judgment, we explore the subject before coming to a decision.

We can also use the PMI as an assessment of any conclusion, decision or problem solution.

We can also use the PMI to help us choose between alternatives, by applying it to each available alternative.

The "interesting" part of the PMI scan opens up possibilities and speculations and leads on to creative thinking.

AGO: Aims, Goals and Objectives

What is the objective of the thinking?

What do we want to achieve?

What do we want to end up with?

The AGO directs attention to the specific purpose of the thinking.

If we know exactly where we want to go, we are more likely to get there.

CAF: Consider All Factors
Look around.
> Explore.
> What factors should he considered in our thinking?
> Have we left out anything?
> What else should be considered?

Before going ahead with the "forward" thinking, let us be sure attention has been paid to all those things that our thinking should take into account.

We have to find the factors ourselves – they are not presented to us as they are in school textbooks.

Real life thinking can be a messy business.

If you leave out important factors, your thinking will never be any good.

OPV: Other People's Views
People are doing the thinking and other people are going to be affected by the thinking.

Let us use the OPV to pay direct attention to all these other people.
> Who are these people?
> What are the views of these people?
> What values are involved?

There are the people who are directly involved or affected by the action that might result from the thinking.

Then there are those who will be affected indirectly.

Should the thinker take these other people into account or just look after his or her own values?

APC: Alternatives, Possibilities and Choices
What are the alternative courses of action?
> What can be done?
> What are the possible solutions?

It is with the APC that we set out to generate possible lines of action.

APC also applies to explanations and perceptions.

With the APC we search through our store of possible alternatives.

What choices do we have?

If we have no alternatives, then we pause and try to construct an alternative.

FIP: First Important Priorities

With the FIP tool we try to see what really matters.

Not everything is equally important.

When we have a clear view of the priorities, we can choose between the various alternatives.

Which alternative best matches the priorities?

Although the priorities are used at this stage of choosing between alternatives, the priorities may have been set up right at the beginning of the thinking after the AGO has been done.

The stricter you are about priorities, the easier decisions become.

C&S: Consequence and Sequel

If we have chosen one alternative as a possible outcome of the thinking, let us see what would happen if we went ahead with the alternative.

What would follow?

What would the results be?

The C&S can also be applied at the decision stage.

By doing a C&S on each alternative we can see which is the best.

The C&S, FIP and the PMI are all tools to help choose between alternatives in decisions and in problem-solving (also in design).

The C&S can be applied directly on its own to any suggested action or initiative.

Critical Thinking

Critical thinking is our check on truth: Is this true?

There are different levels of truth.

There is truth based on experiences of ourselves or of others.

There is checkable truth, when anyone can check what we claim.

Then there is truth based on some authority (science, reference books, etc.).

We need to develop the thinking habit of always asking ourselves: What is the truth value here?

What is important is the level of claimed truth.

This can range from a claimed absolute certainty to something that is only offered as a possibility.

Over-claiming needs to be challenged.

The next role of critical thinking is to check on the logic that is being used.

With logic we seek to derive a further truth from truths which we already have.

We need to ask the habit question:

Does this follow?

With a logical argument, it is claimed that the conclusion must follow from the preceding step.

Very often it is claimed that something must follow because the thinker cannot imagine an alternative.

At the end critical thinking (black-hat thinking) may conclude:

This is false.

This is doubtful.

This is not proven.

This is proven.

Creative Thinking

With creative thinking, we are not so much concerned with proving something as with moving forward with possibilities.

Once we have reached a new idea, we can set about proving its truth and value.

In logical thinking, we seek to move step by logical step from where we are to a new position.

In creative thinking, we can make jumps ahead and when we have reached a new position, we set about checking the value of that position.

Hypothesis, speculation and provocation are all ways of making that creative jump ahead.

Sometimes we have to guess because we do not have enough information for action.

In creative thinking, we guess in order to have new ways of looking at information and in order to explore the possibility of new ideas.

The analysis of information is not sufficient to produce new ideas, because the mind can see only what it is prepared to see – and that means the old ideas.

We need to develop skill in speculation.

Speculation may range from a very reasonable guess (what we seek in a hypothesis) to a mere possibility to a provocation which makes no claim to truth whatever.

The purpose of a provocation is to get us to look at something in a new way – not by presenting the new way but by jerking us out of the old way.

A creative jump ahead can pull our thinking forward.

We lead from in front.

Without creative thinking, we lead from behind and we have to strive to push forward, building on what we know.

The creative attitude involves a willingness to go forward and to explore possibilities.

Lateral Thinking

Lateral thinking is specifically concerned with changing ideas and perceptions.

Attention-directing tools look after the "breadth" aspect of perception.

The lateral-thinking creative tools look after the "change" aspect of perception.

Lateral thinking is based directly on a consideration of the pattern-making behavior of a self-organizing information system (as in perception).

Such systems allow incoming information to organize itself into routine patterns.

Such patterns allow us to function in the world.

We should be grateful for these routine patterns.

But we cannot get across to the available side patterns because of the non-symmetry of patterns.

If we do get across to the side patterns, we have humor or creativity.

All valuable creative ideas must be logical in hindsight but this does not mean they are accessible to logic in the first place.

Two specific techniques are suggested for getting across to these side tracks.

The first technique uses a combination of provocation and movement.

A provocation is an idea that does not exist in experience and has no truth value at all.

We signal such provocation with the invented word "po" to indicate that it is a provocation.

We then use "movement" to move from the routine track to the provocation and then on to the side track (and a new idea).

Movement is different from judgment.

In judgment we compare an idea with what we know and reject the idea if it does not check out.

With movement we operate outside the judgment system.

We look at the idea to see how we can move forward from it.

There are specific methods for setting up provocations: received, reversal, escape, wishful thinking and outrageous.

There are specific methods for obtaining movement from a provocation: attitude, moment-to-moment, extract a principle, focus on the difference and search for values.

These lateral-thinking tools can be practiced and then used deliberately whenever there is a need to generate new ideas.

The Six Thinking Hats

The six thinking hats are somewhere between a tool and a structure for thinking.

They are treated as an attention-directing tool because they direct attention to a "type" or mode of thinking.

The hats can be used individually and separately (occasional use) or in a sequence (systematic use).

White Hat

Information, data, facts and figures.
- What information do we have?
- What information do we not have?
- How can we get this needed information?
- There is a relationship to CAF, OPV and possibly FIP.

Red Hat

Intuition, hunches, feelings and emotions.

A legitimate way to put forward intuition and feelings and to label them as such.
Relationship with values and OPV.

Black Hat
The hat of assessment and checking.
Does what is suggested fit with our experience, our information, the systems, the values and so forth?
The black hat must always be logical and reasons must be given.
Relationship to PMI and C&S.

Yellow Hat
The benefits and the advantages of what is proposed.
The reasons why something can work.
Relationship to C&S and PMI.
Like the black hat, must be logical.

Green Hat
Creativity, action, proposals and suggestions.
This is the generative hat.
Constructive ideas and new ideas.
Direct relationship to APC.

Blue Hat
Overview and control of the thinking process itself.
What are we doing?
What should we do next?
Direct relationship to AGO, focus and purpose, outcome and conclusion.
The hats operate at a much more general level than the perceptual thinking tools.
There is no great advantage in integrating the hats with the other tools.

Further Thinking Habits
Two other aspects of thinking are worth mentioning.

Circumstances

Some truths are universal, but many truths that are claimed as universal apply only under certain circumstances.

This is a common cause of error in thinking and also of many disagreements (because one party is thinking of one set of circumstances and the other party of a different set of circumstances).

Often it is not a matter of arguing whether something is true or not true but of specifying the circumstances under which it is true.

Often both sides in an argument can be right at the same time under different specified circumstances.

So, the thinking habit question is:

Under what circumstances does this apply?

Broad and Detail

This aspect of thinking is part thinking habit and part operation.

We need to get into the habit of carrying out the operation.

There are two habit questions:

What is the broad idea here?

How can this broad idea be carried out in detail?

The ability to move up and down from detail to broad idea and back again is a characteristic of the skilled thinker.

We extract the broad idea in order to change it or to find better ways of carrying it out.

We extract the broad idea in order to simplify things and to understand them better.

When we are generating alternatives, it is usually easier to lay out the broad ideas first.

Then we look to see how these broad ideas could be put into practice as detailed ideas.

Working at the level of "broad ideas" is similar to working at the level of "concept" or "function".

Pedagogical Aspects

Illustration

The purpose of the lesson is made clear by illustration rather than explanation. Examples can be given by illustration.

Practice
This is the most important aspect of the lesson. Only a short time is allowed for each practice item (2–4 minutes). The practice items are given in the lesson notes but may be supplemented by the teacher. However, the teacher should not be too eager to devise other practice items because there are many aspects of these items that have been carefully worked out. The occasional substitution of a new item for an obviously inappropriate one, or the insertion of an item of local interest are to be encouraged – but not wholesale alteration.

Groups
The students work on the practice items in small groups. In many schools, the CoRT thinking lessons are the only occasion for group work of this sort. Depending on the size of the class, there should be four to five students per group. If the total number of groups in the class is more than six, there will not be time to take plenary feedback from all of them, and some random selection will need to occur. Groups should be of mixed ability.

Discussion
Directly or indirectly, discussion must be the most widely used method of teaching thinking. Youngsters are asked to discuss (or write essays on) a problem situation. The aim is to provide practice in thinking. The teacher notes and comments on faults and inappropriate uses of evidence, hoping that students will extract from these clues some general principles of thinking, which they will then use in future, unrelated situations.

Feedback
At the end of the allotted time, the teacher asks for feedback from the group. This may be provided by an appointed group spokesperson or by members speaking as individuals. There are various techniques for feedback: Each group gives one idea, one group gives its whole output and others add new points and so on. The teacher may want to list the ideas on the board. This feedback aspect is very important but difficult. It can take up

too much of the lesson time but students want to have their ideas listened to. The teacher needs to develop a repertoire of responses to give value to each contribution without suggesting there is only one right answer. Some teachers find this open-ended style of teaching easy; others have more difficulty. Others are uncomfortable without the authority of a book of right answers to follow. The teacher can comment on, build up, relate and link together the ideas offered, but only as a fellow thinker, not with any implication that his or her thinking is better because of their teacher status.

Drawing

This is a powerful and practical method of exercising thinking skills, useful with children of different ages, abilities and cultures. It may be used with children as young as five years old and all the way up to adults. With the young children the drawing may be rather rudimentary and may need to be accompanied by teacher questioning and explanation.

These drawings are functional drawings which show how something can be done. In that sense they are problem-solving. There is something to be achieved and the drawing shows how it can be achieved. The drawing may show how you might weigh an elephant, or it might show a machine to exercise dogs.

Transfer

Many thinking skills programs have struggled with the issue of transfer to school achievement and everyday life. However, the thinking that takes place in CoRT is directly about problems in real-life situations, which are drawn from the students' own experience. Through careful selection and the mixture of practice items, children come to realize that thinking skills can be applied to a wide range of situations. When children take their newly acquired skills home and apply them to their parents' problems, transfer to real life is fully contextualized.

Examples of CoRT Activities

What makes a TV or radio program interesting? Do a CAF (Consider All Factors) and then a FIP (First Important Priorities).

Mail services often lose a lot of money, but some areas of their operation might make a profit. If you were running these services, what alternatives might you suggest? (from the APC lesson on Alternatives, Possibilities, Choices).

A father forbids his 13-year-old daughter to smoke. What is his point of view and what is hers? (from the OPV lesson on Other Points of View). Alternatively: a mother forbids her 13-year-old son to take his mobile phone to school.

Multiple solutions to the problem "Which of the following numbers is the exceptional one: 21, 25, 26, 33?":
    21 is exceptional for it has 7 as a factor,
    21 is exceptional for it has 21 as a factor,
    25 is exceptional for it has 5 as a factor,
    25 is exceptional for it has 25 as a factor,
    26 is exceptional for it has 2 as a factor,
    26 is exceptional for it has 13 as a factor,
    26 is exceptional for it has 26 as a factor,
    33 is exceptional for it has 11 as a factor,
    33 is exceptional for it has 33 as a factor,
    25 is exceptional for it is a square number,
    26 is exceptional for it is an even number,
    33 is exceptional for it is greater than 30.

Training for CoRT

Over 300 accredited trainers in 72 counties are accessible via the website https://www.debono.com/training, funneled through 18 Training Partners. This organization provides both in-person and virtual training and facilitation, supported by interactive digital courses and applications, to help you apply the methods to topics that are important to you. Training Partners organize the accreditation of in-house and independent trainers. All Training Partners offer corporate training, and some also provide public workshops. However, many of these are oriented toward delivery to corporate consumers rather than schools. In the UK, Robert Fisher is listed; he can be relied upon to deliver excellent training suitable for schools.

The Six Thinking Hats are for exploring, developing and implementing ideas - and https://www.six-thinking-hats.com/ hosts the online course. Lateral Thinking is a structured approach for thinking differently and https://www.lateralthinking.com/ hosts the online course – some Lateral Thinking challenges can be started with a free trial.

Extensions of CoRT

De Bono reports that his methods have been used around the world by schools and governments, as well as business organizations, including AT&T, British Airways, British Coal, DuPont, Ericsson, Prudential and Siemens. His methods also were used by the organizers of the 1984 Olympic Games in Los Angeles, as well as by the organizers of the 1983 America's Cup.

CoRT was adopted on a large scale by Venezuela, where it was incorporated in the school curriculum. The Venezuelan Minster of Education decided to introduce it into all the elementary schools in the country. Subsequently 42,000 teachers were to be trained to teach thinking skills to 1.2 million Venezuelan school children in grades 4–6. The program has also been used in corrective institutions and detention centers.

References and Bibliography

Daher, W., Tabaja-Kidan, A., & Gierdien, F. (2017). Educating grade 6 students for higher-order thinking and its influence on creativity. *Pythagoras, 38*(1), a350. https://doi.org/10.4102/pythagoras.v38i1.350

De Bono, E. (1969). *The mechanism of mind*. New York: Simon and Schuster.

De Bono, E. (1970). *Lateral thinking*. New York: Harper and Row.

De Bono, E. (1972). *Children solve problems*. Harmondsworth: Penguin Education.

De Bono, E. (1976). *Teaching thinking*. London: Temple Smith.

De Bono, E. (2017). *Teach your child how to think*. Harmondsworth: Penguin.

Edwards, J. (1991). The direct teaching of thinking skills. In Evans, G. (Ed.), *Learning and teaching cognitive skills*. Hawthorn, Victoria: Australian Council for Educational Research.

Hunter-Grundin, E. (1985). *Teaching thinking: An evaluation of Edward de Bono's classroom materials*. London: The Schools Council.

Kumari, S., & Gupta, K. (2014). Effectiveness of creativity training program on concept map performance of secondary school students. *International Journal of Interdisciplinary and Multidisciplinary Studies (IJIMS)*, *1*(5), 127–131. http://www.ijims.com/uploads/aa99d8be704642d4aeb2zppd_569.pdf

Mousa, M. O. (2022). The role of the Cognitive Research Trust (CORT) program as a new instructional model for developing thinking skills. *Journal of Language Studies*, *6*(1), 48–63.

Ritchie, S. M., & Edwards, J. (1996). Creative thinking instruction for aboriginal children. *Learning and Instruction*, *6*(1), 59–75. https://doi.org/10.1016/S0959-4752(96)80004-1

Rule, A. C., & Barrera, M. T. (2006). CoRT thinking skills guide PBL science. *Academic Exchange*, *4*, 145–149.

Turkey, J. A. M. (2019). The impact of using the first and third parts of the CoRT program on the development of critical thinking for talented students in Tafila governorate. *Journal of Studies in Education*, *9*(3), 72–91. https://doi.org/10.5296/jse.v9i3.15020

Zeyad, T. A., & Hameed, D. T. (2022). The effect of CoRT Programme with EFL preparatory school students in writing. *University of Anbar Journal for Humanities*, *19*(4). https://doi.org/10.37653/juah.2022.176886

Section D

Programs Either Within or Outside the Traditional Curriculum

In this section we consider programs that have the flexibility to be used either within a subject or as a separate method or both. Additionally, it will not have escaped the reader that many of the programs previously mentioned had their origins in the last century. To some extent this was inevitable, as it takes many years for programs to build up a solid background of research evidence. However, in this section we come more up-to-date and discuss some programs that originated in the 21st century and can involve the use of digital technology.

11

Philosophy for Children (P4C)

P4C is not about the lives or thoughts of famous philosophers, but about the practical business of enhancing critical and creative thinking – philosophizing. It is a structured pedagogical method that invites and enables children to search for rational and justified answers to important questions that have no simple answers. The theory and practice of P4C owes much to John Dewey and Matthew Lipman and the tradition of reflective education, which puts learning-to-think at the forefront (Dewey, 1997; Lipman et al., 1980). Lipman (1923–2010) conceptualized three modes of thinking (*critical*, *creative* and *caring*) and four main varieties of cognitive skill (*inquiry*, *reasoning*, *concept formation* and *translation*), all of which constitute his definition of philosophical inquiry. A key idea is that philosophy in the classroom should be based upon a "community of inquiry".

P4C capitalizes on children's natural curiosity in order to engage them in a philosophical dialogue; that is, in a deep discussion of questions that have no clear answers and where different points of view can be developed, explained and justified. By engaging in discussion of conflicting points of view, children develop clearer reasons and justifications for their opinions while they also understand how to construct an argument. However, the aims of P4C go beyond the classroom. The Paris Declaration for Philosophy asserted in 1995 that by training free, reflective, minds capable of resisting various forms of propaganda, fanaticism, exclusion and intolerance, philosophical education contributes to peace and prepares everyone to shoulder responsibilities in face of the great challenges of the contemporary world, particularly in the field of ethics.

(UNESCO, 2007, p. xiii)

An ambiguous problem stimulus is offered the class (which could be a story, picture, video clip, poem, etc.). The class discusses what big questions this throws up and decides on one question to pursue. The teacher then models some questions with the class and solicits responses. The class then breaks into pairs or triads to discuss the question further. All report back to a plenary session, where a consensus solution may be identified or several possible solutions outlined. The moral precepts emanating from the question and solutions are explicated and the children are invited to explore these in their everyday life and report back to the start of the next meeting. While usually operating on "big" questions, P4C can also be applied to narrower questions emanating from a subject discipline.

P4C is in use in over 60 countries, including developing nations. It has been used successfully from kindergarten through elementary school and into secondary school, in colleges and universities and in the workplace. P4C is different from other approaches to critical thinking in that it deals with difficult questions that would bewilder many adults, is relevant to any subject or life material, has effects on social and emotional aspects as well as on cognitive development and can be applied outside of school to real-life issues.

Effects of Philosophy for Children

Several evaluations of P4C have been reported by Lipman, including one involving 200 students aged 10–13 who participated for two hours per week over two years. Training of two hours per week was given to the teachers for the first year.

There were effects on intellectual performance, measures of creative and formal reasoning, reading and mathematics.

Two meta-analyses (Trickey and Topping, 2004; Garcia-Moriyon, Robollo and Colom, 2005) showed a consistently high level of effectiveness in terms of cognitive gain, school attainment and socio-emotional enhancement. P4C was found to result in higher performance on tests of cognitive skills compared to a control group both in a primary school in Scotland (Topping and Trickey, 2007a) and in a secondary school in the USA (Fair et al., 2015). In England, P4C primary school pupils in 48 schools over a year showed higher reading and mathematics test scores than control pupils, with disadvantaged students performing best (Gorard, Siddiqui and See, 2017). Not only did thinking skills improve but also attainments in other areas of the curriculum. This is important information to know for teachers who have difficulty justifying the insertion of innovation into their curriculum because of displacement effects on "what has to be covered".

There is evidence that gains from P4C last over time. In Scotland, the primary-school pupils who did P4C went on to a secondary school where they had no such experiences. Nonetheless, their performance on a test of cognitive ability was still well ahead of their control group (Topping and Trickey, 2007b). In Texas, the secondary school pupils who engaged in P4C were tested three years later – again, they, too, showed greater gains than their control group who did not participate (Fair et al., 2015). Remember, this is where P4C had not been done in the follow-up period. So, if teachers really try hard to work on maintenance of gains, they may immunize their students from any unwanted potential effects of later school life to an even greater extent.

P4C can also contribute to the improvement of social and emotional intelligence. This includes:

- Self-Awareness: Knowing how and what you are feeling and how it impacts one's life and having realistic expectations of one's abilities
- Emotional Self-Regulation: Handling emotions so they facilitate the task in hand and having self-imposed boundaries

- Motivation: Having knowledge of motivating factors and forces, having perseverance
- Empathy: Having knowledge of how others are feeling and using that knowledge in interacting with them, having a rapport with a wide variety of people
- Social Skills: Being able to read social situations and using these skills to persuade, lead, negotiate, compromise.

The experience of having one's ideas carefully listened to is likely to strengthen self-esteem and confidence. Children learn to avoid dismissing different views without examining them properly. They learn that they can disagree without falling out. Children may see more clearly the causes of the habitual behavior of others or themselves (e.g., Giménez-Dasí et al., 2017).

Theoretical Underpinnings of Philosophy for Children

P4C develops from Vygotsky's (1962) work, in that the reciprocity between thought and language plays an important role in learning to think. Vygotsky proposed that every feature of a child's cultural development appears twice: first *between* people (*interpsychological*), and then *inside* the child (*intrapsychological*). P4C does not assume that the potential of any child is known in advance – this has to be discovered through interaction. Social construction involves students engaging in group discussion to solve problems or deepen understandings, a necessary feature of thinking skill programs. The majority of students think more productively when they are engaged in groups (Shayer & Adey, 2002).

The process of thinking together is also likely to encourage intrinsic motivation. Students become more intrinsically motivated when their needs for personal autonomy, competence and connection are met (Deci & Ryan, 1985). Collaborative inquiry provides a means of meeting these needs, although this is not its main intention. At any age, intrinsic motivation is seen as more effective than rewards for promoting learning. Topping, Trickey and Cleghorn (2019) discuss theory in more detail.

Structure and Implementation of Philosophy for Children

Teachers may feel that P4C sounds rather scary. First, it implies that the teacher does not know all the right answers but instead is having the students scrutinize his or her thinking. Secondly, it implies that students are able to come up with good rationalizations, something that teachers may doubt; indeed, teachers may wonder whether they themselves would be able to do so. In fact, all these problems go away when you actually conduct P4C. The teacher says straight out at the beginning that she or he doesn't know all the answers – or even any of them. P4C is about the longer-term process of developing better thinking, not about instant better thinking.

Lipman's original materials were a set of mini-novels to be read by pupils, with instruction manuals for teachers. The characters in the novels were children and adolescents figuring out for themselves the laws of reasoning, producing counter-examples and looking for different points of view. Lipman's basic novel was *Harry Stottlemeier's Discovery* (for 8–12-year-olds) with 17 short chapters. Each chapter had a leading idea, such as: the process of inquiry, inference, contradiction, what is a possibility, or causes and effects. The teacher guided students mainly through Socratic questioning.

Of course, there are developmental differences between various age groups, as in kindergarten, lower primary, upper primary, lower secondary, upper secondary, university and college and workplace settings. For example, in kindergarten, the teacher will use a very short and simple story as a stimulus, model a few short questions appropriate to the age of the children, encourage pairs of peers to discuss (for a relatively short time) and have a longer plenary session that is rather more teacher-directed. By contrast, in upper secondary the teacher will use a long, complex and controversial story, video or picture as a stimulus, model a much larger number of much more complex questions, encourage peer discussion for a longer time provided it is constructive, and have a shorter plenary session that is more student-led. Thus, the basic process remains the same across the ages, but it is adapted to the age group in question.

Philosophical dialogue is not just an *exchange* of opinions; rather, it provides a context where students are challenged to *justify* their opinions. Teachers need to leave a space for student speech by their own silence, so that children can articulate exactly what they mean to say. Respectfully listening to student opinions not only supports thoughtful conversations but is highly valued by students.

Teachers might:

- Give students "thinking time"
- Use second questioning
- Scaffold
- Ask all students
- Use careful listening and
- Withhold judgment

Children should:

- Ask open and inviting questions
- Give evidence and examples
- Make comparisons
- Summarize and evaluate and
- Seek clarification

The teacher can help develop the inquiry by:

- Focusing attention on important points
- Encouraging students toward appropriate behaviors (such as how to listen and how to respond to each other)
- Rewarding positive contributions with praise and
- Not being content with mere conversation.

The children should aim to:

- Focus attention on the speaker
- Not "put down" others
- Remember they are not forced to speak
- Respect others' views and
- Be truthful and open-minded

There are other practical elements to consider:

Seating

It is important that the students sit in a position from which they can see each other. Some teachers use a circle, but sometimes this is not possible, so they adopt a semi-circle or horseshoe shape.

Rules

Ground rules are set in advance that encourage showing respect for everyone. Teachers should involve the children in developing the ground rules, so they feel they "own" them.

The Awareness Exercise

This is a simple way of helping children focus full attention (remember, the children may have just been doing something completely different). The noise in the mind subsides. The student becomes mentally, physiologically and emotionally in the best state for thinking and learning. First give your attention to the sense of touch. Feel the weight of your feet on the floor … Your body on the chair … Your clothes on the skin … (Pause) Now, using sight and without naming things in the mind, see colors …. shapes … the space between the shapes. (Pause) Now, using the sense of hearing, hear any sounds close at hand (e.g., within the classroom) … now let the hearing gradually run right out until the furthest sounds can be heard … (Pause) Now try to hold that awareness for a few moments.

The Stimulus

The stimulus is to arouse the interest of the group. It could be a story, poem, picture, brief video, or life incident that introduces a theme from which a philosophical question can be derived that also poses moral dilemmas or raises questions. There is often some ambiguity in it, or something on which there is no clear consensus. The themes might include: Friendship, Helping others, Cooperation, Fairness,

Patience, Sharing, Forgiveness, Freedom, Anger, Beauty, Fear, Bullying, Happiness, Hope or Lies. Aesop's Fables are a very useful initial source for stimuli (see the Library of Congress for examples, http://read.gov/aesop/001.html)

Questioning

Teachers model good questioning by asking for clarification, reasons and evidence (and by inviting the children to first *think* and *then* answer). This provides practice in listening, keeping to the point, assessing assertions and substantiating one's own point of view. The ability to use "good" questions (by teacher or students) is very important. Good questions in this context are questions that are open, that help uncover more about the subject of the dialogue and that build knowledge of it. By using such questions, the dialogue becomes deeper, more meaningful. Questions might be:

- What reasons do you have for saying that? Can you explain more about that? (Clarifying)
- How do you know that? What is your evidence? (Seeking Evidence)
- Is there another point of view? Can you put it in another way? (Exploring Alternative Views)
- Why do you think that? What is the cause of that? (Probing the Superficial)
- If …, then what do you think about …? You said …, but what about …? (Scaffolding)
- How can we test that in practice? Is that consistent with what you first said? (Testing Implications)
- Can anyone summarize the main points for us? Where has our thinking taken us? (Evaluating)

Of course, as the students answer the questions, the teacher comments on the high-quality answers and/or those that lead to more and deeper thoughts. As P4C progresses, children can lead the questioning, building confidence as they learn how to *ask* questions rather than focusing on answering questions.

Peer Work

Students are placed in pairs (or with a group of three if the class has an odd number of students) and asked to discuss their thinking so far. This ensures students understood what was happening in the stimulus and, more importantly, it contains the beginnings of the exploration of ideas from the stimulus. It is also an area for building student confidence. Those who may be unlikely to offer ideas and opinions to the whole class may be confident enough to speak to a peer partner or in a small group. An important role of the teacher here is to circulate and encourage, perhaps scaffolding if appropriate. During this time the peer dialogue moves slowly from the concrete through the personal to the abstract.

Teachers need to be careful that they have enough time to get through all the stages. Of course, the teacher will have made the students aware of the time available at the outset of the stage. This means that as students become more sophisticated and vocal, there may be time pressure and the teacher will need to close out each phase in order to advance to the next. If some discussions still leave a great deal of controversy hanging in the student group, the topic can be returned to in the next session of P4C to seek some kind of resolution.

Query the Justification for Long-Held Beliefs

Students may have learned opinions from their parents or peers without giving them any thought. Also, they can be very vulnerable to false information. The torrent of fake news on various social media makes this even worse. It is easy to believe stories that correspond to existing beliefs. As some politicians have realized, reasoned argument can be less successful than a simple appeal to emotional prejudice. Teachers can take examples of fake news and test them in the course of classroom dialogue. Sometimes students can entertain opposing thoughts without apparent discomfort – P4C drives conceptual change by helping children become more consistent in their thinking.

Develop a Culture of Equal Respect and Participation

A strong school culture of participation and collaboration supports the learning of skills and can lead to enhanced self-esteem and a greater sense of self-efficacy. Participation is a key factor in promoting the emotional well-being of school-age children and the morale of both teachers and students. Participation increases following regular collaborative inquiry. The undivided, unconditional attention of other students is likely to promote positive feelings. Such attention makes students feel worthwhile and understood.

Allow Time to Reorganize Thoughts

When students express their ideas in class, they must organize and process their thoughts. They may discover gaps in their understanding and encounter explanations better than their own. But that means that they don't only have to justify one new thought; they have to reorganize a lot of associated thoughts that were not well justified – a lot to do in response to one question!

Praise Good Examples Among Students

Students are likely to learn from each other during this process. For example, a student might hear another student asking for evidence and then be more likely to internalize this behavior and do the same. Teachers can praise student behavior they hope others will copy.

Don't Be Afraid of Perplexing Questions

Real discussion takes place best when the questions perplex the teacher as well as the students. If the questions chosen for discussion are perplexing for all participants, including the teacher, then communication is likely to be more interactive and more meaningful.

Don't Be Afraid of Controversial Questions

Teachers may feel a little nervous about introducing a topic that could be seen as controversial, whether for political, religious or other reasons. However, these are exactly the kind of questions to generate a heated discussion, so do not shy away from them.

How to Disagree

If someone disagrees, they must find a good reason to express that disagreement (as against simply saying that the other person is "wrong"). Praise pupils who disagree thoughtfully and respectfully.

Community of Inquiry

As time goes on, a "community of inquiry" will be created – a group engaged in exploring ideas through philosophical dialogue, where students think together and build on each other's ideas. In schools the group is usually a class, but it is also possible to use P4C with subgroups within the class at different times. Often the group has evolved its dialogic technique to a degree of sophistication. Participants organize their thinking through questioning, hypothesizing and suggesting alternative explanations. Students justify their views with reasons, drawing inferences, making deductions, identifying underlying assumptions and dealing with contradictions. Reasons and/or evidence clarify ill-defined concepts, avoid sweeping generalizations and inform decisions.

Encouraging Metacognition

Students who are able to reflect on their learning and thinking processes (i.e., show metacognition) are more effective learners than those who are not so able. As students encounter alternative views from other students that are well thought through and have some rational foundation, by a process of comparison this gives them food for thought about the nature of their own thinking (Cam, 2006). As P4C develops, students will increasingly ask themselves about the nature of their utterances before they actually say them. Of course, the whole point of metacognition is that it should not only lead to insights on how you have thought at this moment but should also lead to thoughts and strategies about how you might think better in the future. Thus, as metacognition develops so also should self-regulation of quality of thinking. In this way, children become more effective thinkers in the short term but also develop habits of reflecting on their thinking that are likely to have long-term effects.

Ensuring Effects Last Over Time – Maintenance and Generalization

If teachers really try hard to work on maintenance of gains, they may immunize their students from any unwanted potential effects of later school life to an even greater extent. As part of the ending routine in your regular P4C session, teachers can ask the children to think of their "Thought for the Week" (TftW) – one thought that they will try to apply in and out of school between now and the next P4C session. When the children return to the next P4C session, start by asking for reports on how they applied their TftW. For example, the individual may see there is a difference between his/her thoughts and actions. So, this part of the process reinforces recent learning and relates the theoretical to the real world in which the student lives. Over time, the class will discuss topics that are related to each other. The teacher should ask students what they can remember of a previous session that was related to today's topic. Do they remember some particularly good question or statement from that session? How does it relate to the current topic?

Teachers will feel more confident committing time and energy to philosophical inquiry if improvements in thinking are found to cross subject boundaries, whether planned for or not. Maximizing this generalization of learning beyond the context in which it is learned is crucial (Reznitskaya et al., 2012). Generalization of learning is more likely to occur if activities are constructed to extend that learning to other contexts. Adey and Shayer (see Chapter 2) maximized generalization by building in "bridging" activities. Building in generalization activities was also central to Feuerstein's Instrumental Enrichment program (see Chapter 9).

Ensuring Effects on Adult Life

Citizenship in later adult life requires the ability to discriminate between statements that are rational and factual and those that are not, suspending judgment on those where this is not clear. In 2016, the *Oxford Dictionary* chose "post-truth" as its word of the year, defining it as "relating to or denoting circumstances in which objective facts are less influential in shaping public opinion than appeals to emotion and personal belief". Associated with this we have "fake news", defined by the *Collins English Dictionary* as "false, often sensational information disseminated under the guise of news reporting". False claims are 70% more likely than the truth to be shared on Twitter. True stories take about six times longer than false ones to reach 1,500 people (Vosoughi et al., 2018). It takes a few minutes to create a viral story, but hours of investigative work to debunk it. Never before has critical thinking been so necessary. If students are to become thoughtful analytical members of a participatory democracy, critical thinking will be essential (Di Masi and Santi, 2016).

Use P4C with Hot Topics

Once students are more familiar with P4C, you can unleash them on hot topics such as climate change (see if the geography or social studies teachers are interested!). Does it exist and, if so, what might be done about it?

Use P4C with Topics That are Hot for Pupils

Not all pupils will be excited by such large phenomena as global warming; they may be much more excited by a topic near to their hearts, like "should mobile phones be allowed in schools?"

Use P4C with Habitual Beliefs

Have students identify long-held or habitual beliefs that they used to have, but which they have now changed in the light of new (reliable) information coupled with better thinking. Have them share these with the group, because other students might not yet have changed their minds.

Use P4C to Identify Cognitive Bias

Beliefs tend to be the result of cognitive bias – we all look for information that supports our existing beliefs. See if the students can identify each other's cognitive biases – but this is better done via peer work, or people will feel foolish.

Example of Philosophy for Children Activities

This example was used with a young elementary school class.

Marvin Gets Mad
Possible themes are: anger, patience, loneliness, being sorry, wanting things, can animals have feelings?

Focusing/ Awareness Exercise	Get ready to listen. 1. Gather the class together in a circle. Pass round a "Hello, welcome to our philosophy group". 2. Practice sitting still and connecting with the listening until the class falls quiet. What did they notice? 3. Remind the class of the rules for P4C, particularly listening to each other and "no put-downs".
Stimulus: Story, Poem, Activity	Introduce the story *Marvin Gets Mad*. Look at the cover. What is in the picture? How do you think he is feeling? What do you think the story could be about? (Take different ideas.) Have you ever been mad? Now read the story to the class, enjoying the pictures and talking about facial expressions and feelings as you read, without losing the thread of the story. After reading, recap events in stories with children. Get them to act out facial expressions. How did Marvin feel? e.g., Finding the apple tree (surprised, pleased) Not being able to reach the apple (disappointed) Waiting for the apple to fall (patient) Molly had eaten the apple (disappointed) Marvin getting madder, stamping and shouting "BAAAA" (angry) Ground swallowing him up (surprised) In the hole (lonely) Molly appears (relieved, sorry) Back to everything perfect (happy) Wanted the pear
Think, Pair, Share	Construct questions that students can think about, then talk to a partner about: How do we know when we are angry? How do we know when someone else is angry? What kinds of things make *you* angry? How do you feel after you have been angry? Sorry? Relieved? What? Can you pretend to be angry? Can anger ever be a good thing?

Dialogue/ Discussion Plan	Theme: ANGER Story Why do you think Marvin got mad? How do you think Molly felt when Marvin got mad at her? Why? How do you think the chickens, ducks and cows felt? Why? If you had been Marvin, would you have gotten mad? What would you have done? Personal Have you ever been angry like Marvin? (*Take examples*) What does it feel like? Can you stop being angry if you want to? How do you feel if someone is angry at you? Are you ever sorry after you have been angry? Why? Do you ever pretend to be angry? Philosophical Can anger be a good thing? When? What is anger?
What have we talked about?	What did we talk about today? How well did we do in our thinking and talking? (Use thumbs up or down to show) Whose partner had a really good thought? What made it a really good thought?
Thought for the week	This week think about being angry. What makes you angry? What happens when we get angry? Can we stop being angry? Come back next week to tell us what you have thought – and done.

Training for Philosophy for Children

Philosophy for Children is now a worldwide network. The International Council of Philosophical Enquiry with Children (ICPIC) (https://www.icpic.org) lists 60 countries as members, and enquirers may contact any of these for information about training in that country. In the UK, SAPERE (Society for the Advancement of Philosophical Enquiry) (https://www.sapere.org.uk) offers training courses for teachers. There are one or two university courses devoted to P4C (e.g., the P4C course at the University of Strathclyde, Glasgow). Topping (2022) has described a training course for teachers that operates on an online basis and could be accessed from anywhere in the world.

There are also a number of journals devoted to this field. *Thinking: The Journal of Philosophy for Children* was published until

2014 by Montclair University. Past issues are available online at https://www.montclair.edu/iapc/thinking-the-journal-of-philosophy-for-children. The *Journal of Philosophy in Schools* has a strong focus on P4C (https://jps.bham.ac.uk). Other relevant journals have a wider scope than P4C: *Thinking Skills and Creativity* (https://www.sciencedirect.com/journal/thinking-skills-and-creativity/), *Thinking and Reasoning* (https://www.tandfonline.com/toc/ptar20/current/) and the *Journal of Philosophy of Education* (https://academic.oup.com/jope/pages/about/).

Extensions of Philosophy for Children

P4C is used in many countries and many languages, with very young children right through to elderly adults. Mostly it occupies a separate session in the school curriculum each week, with associated bridging activities to help children connect it to other subjects and contexts, but sometimes it occupies the lesson of another subject and focuses on problems in that subject. Sometimes it operates as a before- or after-school club. Sometimes it operates out of school. There is very little that you cannot do with P4C.

References and Bibliography

Cam, P. (2006). *20 thinking tools*. Camberwell, Australia: ACER Press.

Deci, E. L., & Ryan, R. M. (1985). *Intrinsic motivation and self-determination in human behavior*. New York, NY: Plenum Press.

Dewey, J. (1997). *How we think*. Mineola, NY: Dover Publications.

Di Masi, D., & Santi, M. (2016). Learning democratic thinking: A curriculum to Philosophy for Children as citizens. *Journal of Curriculum Studies*, *48*(1), 136–150. https://doi.org/10.1080/00220272.2015.1088064

Fair, F., Haas, L. E., Gardosik, C., Johnson, D. D., Price, D. P., & Leipnik, O. (2015). Socrates in the schools from Scotland to Texas: Replicating a study on the effects of a Philosophy for Children program. *Journal of Philosophy in Schools*, *2*(1), 18–37. https://doi.org/10.21913/jps.v2i1.1100

Garcia-Moriyon, F., Robollo, I., & Colom, R. (2005). Evaluating Philosophy for Children: A meta-analysis. *Thinking*, *17*(4), 14–22. https://doi.org/10.5840/thinking20051743

Giménez-Dasí, M., Quintanilla, L., Ojeda, V., & Lucas Molina, B. (2017). Effects of a dialogue-based program to improve emotion knowledge in Spanish Roma preschoolers. *Infants and Young Children*, *30*(1), 3–16. https://doi.org/10.1097/IYC.0000000000000086

Gorard, S., Siddiqui, N., & See, B. H. (2017). Can Philosophy for Children improve primary school attainment? *Journal of Philosophy of Education*, *51*(1), 5–22. https://doi.org/10.1111/1467-9752.12227

Lipman, M., Sharp, A., & Oscanyan, F. (1980). *Philosophy in the classroom*. Philadelphia, PA: Temple University Press.

Reznitskaya, A., Glina, M., Carolan, B., Michaud, O., Rogers, J., & Sequeira, L. (2012). Examining transfer effects from dialogic discussions to new tasks and contexts. *Contemporary Educational Psychology*, *37*(4), 288–306. https://doi.org/10.1016/j.cedpsych.2012.02.003

Shayer, M., & Adey, P. (2002). (Eds.) *Learning intelligence: Cognitive acceleration across the curriculum from 5 to 15 years*. Buckingham: Open University Press.

Topping, K. J. (2022). Training Philosophy for Children facilitators via technology and peer assessment. In A. Kizel (Ed.), *Philosophy with children and teacher education: Global perspectives on critical, creative and caring thinking* (pp. 95–103). London & New York: Routledge. https://www.routledge.com/Philosophy-with-Children-and-Teacher-Education-Global-Perspectives/Kizel/p/book/9781032080574

Topping, K. J. (2023). Cooperative learning through Philosophy for Children around the world. In R. Gillies, B. Millis, & N. Davidson (Eds.), *Contemporary global perspectives on cooperative learning* (pp. 144–156). London & New York: Routledge.

Topping, K. J., & Trickey, S. (2007a). Collaborative philosophical enquiry for school children: Cognitive gains at two-year follow-up. *British Journal of Educational Psychology*, *77*(4), 787–796. https://doi.org/10.1348/000709906X105328

Topping, K. J., & Trickey, S. (2007b). Collaborative philosophical enquiry for school children: Cognitive effects at 10–12 years. *British Journal of Educational Psychology*, *77*, 271–288. https://doi.org/10.1348/000709906X105328

Topping, K. J., & Trickey, S. (2015). The role of dialogue in Philosophy for Children. In L. B. Resnick, C. S. C. Asterhan, & S. N. Clarke (Eds.), *Socializing intelligence through academic talk and dialogue.* (pp. 99–110). Washington, DC. American Educational Research Association and Rowman & Littlefield.

Topping, K. J., Trickey, S., & Cleghorn, P. (2019). *A teacher's guide to Philosophy for Children.* New York and London: Routledge. Resources website: www.routledge.com/9781138393264

Topping, K. J., Trickey, S., & Cleghorn, P. (2020). *Philosophy for Children.* Educational Practices Series #32. Geneva: International Bureau of Education, United Nations Educational, Scientific and Cultural Organisation (UNESCO) and Brussels: International Academy of Education (IAE) (also in Spanish, Chinese, French, German, Portuguese, Catalan, Hungarian, Russian, Urdu, Arabic, Polish, Japanese, Marathi, Hindi). Available: http://www.ibe.unesco.org/en/news/philosophy-children-educational-practices-series-32-0

Trickey, S., & Topping, K. J. (2004). "Philosophy for Children": A systematic review. *Research Papers in Education, 19*(3), 363–378. https://doi.org/10.1080/0267152042000248016

Trickey, S., & Topping, K. J. (2006). Collaborative philosophical enquiry for school children: Socio-emotional effects at 11–12 years. *School Psychology International, 27*(5), 599–614. https://doi.org/10.1177/0143034306073417

Trickey, S., & Topping, K. J. (2007). Collaborative philosophical enquiry for school children: Participant evaluation at 11 years. *Thinking: The Journal of Philosophy for Children, 18*(3), 23–34. https://doi.org/10.5840/thinking20071835

United Nations Educational, Scientific and Cultural Organization (2007). *Philosophy. A school of freedom: Teaching philosophy and learning to philosophize: Status and prospects.* Paris: UNESCO.

Vosoughi, S., Roy, D., & Aral, S. (2018). The spread of true and false news online. *Science,* 359, 6380, 1146–1151. https://doi.org/10.1126/science.aap9559

Vygotsky, L. S. (1962). *Thought and language.* Cambridge, MA: MIT Press.

12
Problem-Based Learning (PBL)

Problem-Based Learning is a learner-centered approach that empowers learners to work in cooperative groups to conduct research, integrate theory and practice and different disciplines and apply knowledge and skills to develop a viable solution to a problem that will have unclear and/or multiple solutions.

PBL was developed in medical education at McMaster University in Canada, where it became apparent that traditional lecture methods might increase knowledge but did little in terms of synthesis and application of that knowledge in a clinical setting. It then spread to medical education in many parts of the world. Movement into school education is much more recent and even now most PBL applications are in secondary schools rather than elementary schools.

There are other closely related learner-centered instructional strategies, such as project-based learning, case-based learning and inquiry-based learning. Project-based learning is similar to PBL in that the learning activities are organized around achieving a shared goal (project). However, learners are usually provided with specifications for a desired end product and the learning process is more oriented to following correct procedures. Cases and projects tend to diminish the learner's role in setting the goals and outcomes for the problem. Another primary difference relates to the role of the tutor. In an inquiry-based approach, the tutor is both a facilitator of learning and a provider of information. In PBL the tutor supports the process and expects learners to make their thinking clear but does not provide information related to the problem – that is the responsibility of the learners.

Nagarajan and Overton (2019) helpfully described a number of "System Thinking" skills that might be developed by PBL: "forest thinking" (understanding the behavior of the system as a whole), "closed-loop thinking" (considering the effect of system-relevant variables on each other), "system-as-cause thinking" (evaluating internal causes of the system's behavior) and "operational thinking" (identifying variables that influence a system's behavior and its changes).

Most state-funded elementary schools, middle schools and high schools are constrained by a state-mandated curriculum and an expectation that they will produce a uniform product. High-stakes standardized testing tends to support instructional approaches that teach to the test. These approaches focus primarily on memorization through drill and practice and rehearsal using practice tests. PBL offers a different way, with an emphasis on interdisciplinary and applied work, but may be difficult to fit into the existing school structure.

Problems in the real world are ill-structured (or they would not be problems). A critical skill developed through PBL is the ability to identify the problem and set parameters on the development of a solution. Key issues for the teacher are the selection of ill-structured problems and their role in guiding the learning process and conducting a thorough debriefing at the conclusion of the learning experience. The skills developed by PBL include the ability to think critically, analyze and solve complex, real-world problems, find, evaluate, and use appropriate learning resources, work cooperatively, demonstrate effective communication skills and use content knowledge and intellectual skills.

However, critics have pointed out that implementation of PBL can be time-consuming (for both students and instructor) and dependent on expensive resources that may not always be available. Educators also report that students who do not have the necessary academic preparation may find the PBL exercise overwhelming.

There are many studies of PBL in higher education and in the professions, but rather fewer in schools and most of these are in secondary schools, although a book by Torp and Sage (2002) began to dispel this situation.

Effects of Problem-Based Learning

There are four reviews or meta-analyses of PBL, but the vast majority of studies in them took place in higher education. Dochy et al. (2003) examined 43 studies and found there was a robust positive effect from PBL on the skills of students, shown by vote count (how many studies found in favor of BL) as well as by effect size. Effect Sizes were 0.46 for skills and 0.22 for knowledge. No single study reported negative effects. However, there was some evidence that a considerable increase in skills capability might be coupled with a decline in knowledge relative to control groups. This might be expected as PBL students did not have time to absorb and memorize as much knowledge. However, this result was strongly influenced by just two outlier studies. Also, while students in PBL gained slightly less knowledge, they remembered more of that knowledge – studies using a follow-up retention period tended to find more positive effects. In addition, the year level of the student was associated with variation in effect sizes, but not consistently. A wide range of different kinds of assessment were deployed. The more an instrument was capable of evaluating the skills of the student, the larger the effect of PBL.

A year later, Hmelo-Silver (2004) published a review, noting that PBL argued for the importance of practical, meaningful, experiential learning. Working together, students identified facts relevant to the problem scenario, generated hypotheses and identified what necessary information was not known, applied the new knowledge and ended with a problem solution and the ability to generalize that to other similar situations. Much of the evidence came from medical schools, although there were a few studies involving other populations. There were many innovative descriptions of using PBL in various settings: educational administration, business, educational psychology, engineering, chemistry, various undergraduate disciplines and K–12 education. Hmelo-Silver found that there was little research with K–12 populations and much of the research had used case study, pre–post-test or quasi-experimental designs rather than controlled experiments.

A further year later, Gijbels et al. (2005) published a follow-up to Dochy et al.'s meta-analysis. This investigated the influence of assessment on the reported effects of problem-based learning (PBL). Three levels of the knowledge structure that could be targeted by assessment of problem solving were used as the main independent variables: (a) understanding of concepts, (b) understanding of the principles that link concepts and (c) linking of concepts and principles to conditions and procedures for application. PBL had the most positive effects when the focal constructs being assessed were at the level of understanding principles that link concepts. The results suggest that the implications of assessment must be considered in examining the effects of problem-based learning and probably in all comparative education research.

Forty studies met the inclusion criteria for the meta-analysis – 31 (77%) presented data on knowledge-concepts effects, 17 (42%) presented data on knowledge-principles effects and 8 (20%) presented data on effects concerning the application of knowledge (conditions and procedures). Three studies were serious outliers. When these three studies (all situated at the concept level of the knowledge structure) were left aside, the main effects of PBL on the three levels of the knowledge structure measured appeared to be different. The Concepts Effect Size (ES) was not significant, Principles was ES = 0.80 and Application was ES = 0.34. The results suggested that students in PBL perform better at the second and third levels of the knowledge structure. None of the studies reported significant negative findings.

Finally, in 2011 Masek and Yamin offered a further review, including experimental studies from multiple disciplines between the years 2000 to 2011. Again, almost all studies were in higher education and there were still questions about the effectiveness of PBL with a school population. PBL processes certainly theoretically supported students' critical thinking development, but empirical evidence in schools was too limited to form conclusions. It might be that longer-term exposure to PBL was needed to foster students' critical thinking ability.

However, this review was not able to access more recent studies of PBL in schools. Many individual studies can now be found demonstrating the positive effects of PBL in schools. A list of examples will be found in Appendix 2.

Theoretical Underpinnings of Problem-Based Learning

As we have noted above, PBL originated in medical education, with an intention to focus on the multi-disciplinary applied solution of real problems rather than amassing subject knowledge learned in silos. The theoretical underpinnings are not explicit, although a link to the views of Dewey is evident. Insofar as PBL involves collaboration, dialogue and scaffolding between peers, social constructivism is clearly relevant.

Hmelo-Silver (2004) argued that the concept of "learning by doing" in the PBL approach is supported by Experiential Learning Theory, which essentially says that the best way to learn things is by actually having experiences. Those experiences then stick in your mind and help you retain information, facts and skills. PBL also features situated cognition. The context in which learning takes place is critical and skills and concepts should not be taught independently of their real-world context and situation.

Some researchers would say that PBL is a form of cognitive apprenticeship, like traditional apprenticeships, in which the apprentice learns a trade such as tailoring or woodworking by working under a master teacher. Cognitive apprenticeships allow masters to model behaviors in a real-world context. After listening to the master explain exactly what they are doing and thinking as they model the skill, the apprentice identifies relevant behaviors and develops a conceptual model of the processes involved. The apprentice then attempts to imitate those behaviors as the master observes and coaches. However, there is no "master" in PBL, as the teacher's role is not to give information.

Structure and Implementation of Problem-Based Learning

Discussing problems in a PBL group (before beginning to research learning issues) activates relevant prior knowledge and facilitates the processing of new information. Students are better able to construct new knowledge when they can relate it to what they already know.

PBL practitioners suggest class action research has four main stages: planning, implementation, observation and, lastly, reflection. The lesson plan includes: (1) preliminary activities covering the phenomena in everyday life, questions to explore the initial knowledge of students and the delivery of learning objectives; (2) the core activities covering the learning stages of the PBL; and (3) closing activities that consist of a review of the group outcomes and the learning conclusions. During reflection the students analyze the learning process implemented and discuss the constraints that occurred during the learning process and their potential solutions. The results of analysis and discussion are used to improve the implementation of the learning process in the next cycle.

The nature of questioning and the balance between teacher and student questioning is an interesting issue in PBL. One study categorized questions into high order, low order, eliciting ideas and evaluating ideas questions. Findings showed that the percentage of student questions was 68% while for teacher questions it was 32%. The amount of student questions per hour was relatively high at 8.2 questions per student. Nearly half of the classroom questions were low order questions (48%), such as clarification, verification, concept completion, disjunctive, definition, example, quantification and feature specification questions. Higher order questions made up 16%, which included causal antecedent, causal consequence, goal orientation, comparison, enablement and reflective questions. Eliciting ideas questions raised by the teacher covered 9% while evaluating ideas questions by students covered 27%.

Achieving the development of effective problem-solving skills includes the ability to apply appropriate reasoning strategies. For example, hypothetical-deductive reasoning is an appropriate strategy for medical problem solving, whereas analogical or case-based reasoning may be more appropriate in other design domains such as architecture.

Collaborative problem-solving groups are a key feature of PBL. The small group structure helps distribute the cognitive load among members of the group, taking advantage of group members' distributed expertise by allowing the whole group to tackle problems that would normally be too difficult for each student alone. The notion of distributed expertise is particularly relevant in PBL, because the students divide up the learning issues as they become "experts" in particular topics. Furthermore, the small group discussions and debate in PBL sessions enhance problem solving and higher order thinking and promote shared knowledge construction.

Being a good collaborator means knowing how to function well as part of a team. This encompasses establishing common ground, resolving discrepancies, negotiating the actions that a group is going to take and coming to an agreement. These tasks require an open exchange of ideas and engagement by all members of the group. Explaining one's ideas is important for productive collaboration and also serves to enhance learning. The goal of becoming a good collaborator and the process of learning collaboratively are often woven together.

Students are more motivated when they believe that the outcome of learning is under their control. To be intrinsically motivating, problems should provide students with the goal of applying their knowledge to solve a concrete problem. This type of goal is more motivating than more distant, abstract goals that may seem insurmountable. Classroom contexts that reward students for deep understanding, independent thought and action are also more motivating than many traditional classroom structures that reward comparative performances.

Whiteboards can be very useful for compiling and categorizing emerging ideas in PBL. For example, while determining the cause of a chemical spill, the whiteboard was divided into four record-keeping columns to facilitate problem solving. The Facts column held information that the students gleaned from the problem statement (such as what the problem was and where it occurred). The Ideas column served to keep track of evolving hypotheses about solutions, such as reducing the storage of hazardous chemicals. The students placed their questions for further study into the Learning Issues column. Students used the Action Plan column to keep track of plans for resolving the problem or obtaining additional information, such as calling a government agency.

At several points during their problem solving, students typically pause to reflect on the data they have collected so far, generate questions about those data and hypothesize about underlying causal mechanisms that might help explain the data. Students also identify concepts they need to learn more about in order to solve the problem.

To foster flexible thinking, problems need to be complex, ill-structured and open-ended. To support intrinsic motivation, they must also be realistic and resonate with the students' experiences. A good problem affords feedback that allows students to evaluate the effectiveness of their knowledge, reasoning and learning strategies. The problems should also promote conjecture and argumentation. Problem solutions should be complex enough to require many interrelated pieces and should motivate the students' need to know and learn. As students generate hypotheses and defend them to others in their group, they publicly articulate their current state of understanding, enhancing knowledge construction and setting the stage for future learning.

The PBL facilitator (a) guides the development of higher order thinking skills by encouraging students to justify their thinking and (b) externalizes self-reflection by directing appropriate questions to individuals. Although the facilitator fades some of his/her scaffolding as the group gains experience with the PBL method, s/he continues to monitor the group, making moment-to-moment decisions about how best to facilitate the PBL process.

Reflecting on the relationship between problem solving and learning is a critical component of PBL and is needed to support the construction of extensive and flexible knowledge. This reflection should help learners understand the relationship between their learning and problem-solving goals. Thus, each problem-solving task is not an end in itself, but rather a means to achieve a self-defined learning goal. Reflection helps students (a) relate their new knowledge to their prior understanding, (b) mindfully abstract knowledge and (c) understand how their learning and problem-solving strategies might be reapplied.

The literature on transfer shows that individuals have a difficult time transferring general principles from one task to another, even when the knowledge is relevant to someone who understands both tasks. Reflection should increase the probability of transfer.

In the final stage, students prepare for a project presentation and assessment. Students present their proposal of a solution. The facilitator evaluates students' work based on either group or individual presentation. In some cases, peer assessment is used to modify the group's mark. Other methods of assessment are also employed in monitoring students' progress in learning.

PBL should help students improve their creative thinking ability. Creative thinking is a thinking process characterized by fluency, flexibility, originality and elaboration. Fluency is the ability to express ideas clearly. Flexibility is the ability to generate a variety of ideas from different standpoints. Originality is the ability to offer unique or unusual ideas, different from those in books or peculiar from the opinions of others. Elaboration is the ability to explain the influencing factors and to add detail to the ideas at hand as to make them much more valuable.

Turning to digital technologies, one study involved a course website and audio-recording software. Before the semester started, the instructor searched for an appropriate online teaching platform. The content management system, XOOPS (eXtensible Object Oriented Portal System), was adopted as the course website. XOOPS is an open-source framework and provides functions of user management, anonymous discussion forum, file downloading, file uploading, website links and group management (see official website at: http://xoops.org). The course website mainly consisted of four sections: course information, course content, course discussion and student system. "Course information" provided course description, syllabus, assignments, grading and course-related information; "course content" included the audio files and the examples for students' exercises. Students could download the files and listen to the recording via the website to review or complete exercises repeatedly. The instructor could ask questions in the course discussion board in order to promote discussion and interaction between students and himself. The enhancement of students' computing skills in terms of their average grades on three modules (Word, Excel, and PowerPoint) in the PBL class (67.48) was significantly higher than that in the non-PBL class (57.00). That is, in a web-enabled learning environment, the effects of problem-based learning on enhancing students' computing skills may be positive, and higher than of those without PBL.

Examples of Problem-Based Learning Activities

Students were required to apply for a job as marketing assistant for an online-game company. They were required to design and then build autobiographies and résumés by applying computing skills they had just learned. In the Excel module, students played roles as if they were employed by this same software company, and a marketing manager asked them to compare expenses resulting from different distribution channels. Then they had to survey data and complete a worksheet with graphs to contrast the differences between channels. Additionally, they had to come up with a recommendation regarding the best combination of channels. In the last module, they were promoted to marketing managers. They were asked to develop a business proposal for a new online game. They had to present this proposal with visual aids to convince the managing director to enter the market, so a persuasive PowerPoint was built.

The importance of water quality can be taught through PBL. The instructor introduces the topic by (1) talking about access to pure drinking water as a global problem and how humans interact with/influence the water cycle and (2) enabling students to connect water quality to pollutants and consider the role of the environment in this problem. A systems thinking approach asks students to consider that water quality is determined by environmental factors, quantity and type of pollutants, which can be liquids, solids and dissolved substances or particulates (operational thinking). Students analyze the effect of a number of compounds/ions, nitrates, nitrites, phosphates, ammonia and ammonium on the quality of water. Students can measure the concentration of nutrients to understand their impact on water quality (quantitative thinking). A change in concentration of various nutrients will affect quality of water (system-as-cause thinking). Water quality also depends on physical parameters, climate and rainfall (dynamic thinking) and is impacted by temperature and amount of dissolved oxygen. Students can deduce, through experimentation, that the amount of dissolved oxygen in water decreases as temperature increases (closed-loop thinking). Water quality can be influenced by the presence of wetlands, which enhance water quality by acting as filters, and removing pollutants (forest thinking).

PBL can also be used to explore "if bottled water is worth buying" and if bottled water is superior to tap water. Students must be able to identify factors that decide the quality of bottled water. Students have to consider contradictory results that report that minerals in bottled water have medicinal and therapeutic effects, and other studies that suggest that components in bottled water interfere with endocrine activity. Using inductively coupled plasma mass spectrometry (ICPMS), students analyze samples from different sources: natural spring water, distilled water, municipal tap water and well water. Results obtained by students should indicate that untreated municipal tap water and untreated well water have a higher concentration of sodium compared to bottled water samples. In addition, bottled water samples have a lower concentration of magnesium compared to municipal tap and well water samples. Students also concluded that use of a reverse osmosis system reduced concentration of mineral elements. Results from experiments indicated that the major difference between samples was dependent on hardness and taste. Students then presented their results in the form of a poster presentation.

PBL can also focus on sustainable development, exploring the unifying role of chemistry in developing renewable energy sources, recycling and atom economy. Students were asked to assist and advise a company on efficient use of energy and technology in four different scenarios, each with a defined budget. The first scenario required students to advise on the design of a sustainable village with 60% of the raw materials sourced locally, while minimizing the environmental impact of construction. Students had to think critically, balancing requirements and costs while minimizing the impact on the environment. The second scenario required students to design a self-sustaining graduate school in a mountain environment. This activity required students to focus on the use of renewable energy, the minimization of waste and attention paid to the nature of building materials used. The third scenario required students to analyze the cost of producing biodiesel and bioethanol to power a fleet of buses. Students had to evaluate the feasibility of construction of a bioethanol fermentation plant and biodiesel processing plant, and evaluate costs of reactants, fuel mixtures, production and implementation. The final scenario required students to help a university become greener, which involved consideration of many issues including recycling, energy use and waste management.

PBL has been used to teach students about radioactive waste disposal, focusing on low level radioactive waste (LLRW) and enabling students to see connections between science, law and ethics and the underlying role of chemistry in decision-making processes. Students worked together in groups to make a policy decision about disposal of LLRW by gathering information on their own. PBL helped students realize the interdisciplinary nature of physical and biological sciences by integrating concepts such as biological effects of radiation, risk analysis, biological half-life and ethics. It equipped students with knowledge for making informed decisions on LLRW in their communities.

A number of studies in schools have used digital technology, either to extend interactions outside of the classroom or to provide richer media than the students might ordinarily access, or both. However, the technology merely affords the possibility of working anytime from anywhere, rather than fundamentally affecting the pedagogy involved. For instance, one study used a virtual laboratory, an interactive multimedia-based software that contained laboratory equipment that could simulate lab work. Students taught via the PBL model had a higher score for in-depth processing, gradual processing, self-regulation and external regulation in independent learning, compared to students who studied with a lecture-based curriculum.

Another study used a computer-based algebrator with PBL to extend students' understanding of algebra. Algebrators will solve any equation you enter and show you steps and explanations (see https://softmath.com). The PBL classes were given ill-structured tasks as homework that demanded their visiting the libraries and surfing the net in preparation for presentation in the next contact period. The PBL involved three phases, namely: pre-computer session – in which word problems were broken down and translated into algebraic symbols; computer session – in which the algebrator software was used to solve algebraic problems; and post-computer session – in which participants were evaluated through assignments given online and submitted via email.

Training for Problem-Based Learning

Remarkably few studies offer much detail about the training of the teachers prior to commencing PBL, or about the training of the students by the teachers. It seems that much of the "training" occurs as the students progress through the problem. An exception to this was the study of Ojaleye and Awofala (2018) in mathematics, particularly algebra. First, the mathematics teachers were given a comprehensive orientation on the principles behind PBL. They were free to ask questions and offer suggestions on how best this approach might be successfully implemented. The teachers were trained for a period of two hours per week for two weeks on the use of PBL, after which they were assessed through a micro-teaching exercise in the preparation of the PBL lesson. Each of the trained teachers then led the teaching of the students in their respective schools, using the PBL instructional strategy and seeking to ensure fidelity of treatment.

Before the actual implementation, each participating teacher ensured that the participants in their schools had email addresses and the class email address. The PBL involved three phases: pre-computer session – in which a word problem was broken down and translated into algebraic symbols; computer session – in which the algebrator software was used to solve an algebraic problem; and post-computer session – in which participants were evaluated through an assignment given online and submission via email.

In a 12-week PBL exercise, weeks 1–3 involved: selection and training of research assistants on the administration of instruments, selection of schools, categorization of schools into experimental and control groups, random selection of intact classes; selection, sensitization and training of participating teachers; administration of measurement instrument as pre-test on both the experimental and control groups. Weeks 4–11 involved: implementation of training packages in experimental and control schools, that is, teaching in the experimental and control schools using lesson plans on PBL in schools. In the PBL group, participants were exposed to the algebrator supplemented with email. The topics considered include factorization, quadratic equations, rational fractions, simultaneous equations and graphs. Week 12 involved: administration of the post-test measure on both the experimental and control groups.

Torp and Sage (2002) provide several examples of PBL in K-12 education, although this study is not accompanied by any evaluation.

Extensions of Problem-Based Learning

We have noted that PBL can be applied to any subject area, but that one of its virtues is that it enables multi-disciplinarity – working across subjects. While multi-disciplinary projects are common in elementary schools, in secondary schools the framework of subjects militates against this, which is perhaps why there are so many studies of PBL in secondary schools. More studies in elementary schools would certainly be welcome. Additionally, PBL has been used in many very different countries, initially in medical education, but now increasingly in secondary and elementary schools. It seems acceptable to many different cultures.

PBL has also been used in online and blended environments by deploying a variety of digital tools and this may increase in the future, but the essential pedagogy will remain the same. The chief obstacle to wholly online PBL (which would enable PBL between countries, for example) is access to a shared digital whiteboard for jointly recording and categorizing ideas as they emerge, but Google Docs (for example) supports such a function without any cost.

References and Bibliography

Dochy, F., Segers, M., Van den Bossche, P., & Gijbels, D. (2003). Effects of problem-based learning: A meta-analysis. *Learning and Instruction*, *13*, 533–568. https://doi.org/10.1016/S0959-4752(02)00025-7

Gijbels, D., Dochy, F., van den Bossche, P., & Segers, M. (2005). Effects of problem-based learning: A meta-analysis from the angle of assessment. *Review of Educational Research Spring*, *75*(1), 27–61. https://doi.org/10.3102/00346543075001027

Hmelo-Silver, C. E. (2004). Problem-based learning: What and how do students learn? *Educational Psychology Review*, *16*(3), 235–266. https://doi.org/10.1023/B:EDPR.0000034022.16470.f3

Masek, A., & Yamin, S. (2011). The effect of problem based learning on critical thinking ability: A theoretical and empirical review. *International Review of Social Sciences and Humanities*, *2*(1), 215–221.

Nagarajan, S., & Overton, T. (2019). Promoting systems thinking using project- and problem-based learning. *Journal of Chemical Education*, *96*, 2901–2909. https://doi.org/10.1021/acs.jchemed.9b00358

Ojaleye, O., & Awofala, A. O. A. (2018). Blended learning and problem-based learning instructional strategies as determinants of senior secondary school students' achievement in algebra. *International Journal of Research in Education and Science*, *4*(2), 486–501. ERIC Number: EJ1185068

Savery, J. R. (2006). Overview of problem-based Learning: Definitions and distinctions. *Inter-disciplinary Journal of Problem-Based Learning*, *1*(1). https://doi.org/10.7771/1541-5015.1002

Torp, L., & Sage, S. (2002). *Problems as possibilities: Problem-based learning for K-12 education* (2nd ed.). Alexandria, VA: Association for Supervision and Curriculum Development.

13

Educational Games

Computerized educational games are designed to help people learn about certain or many subjects, expand concepts, reinforce development, understand a historical event or culture, or assist them in learning a skill as they play, but do so within the context of a game that has rules and clear objectives (e.g., to "win"). They can be "serious" games designed especially for their educational value, or commercial games that nonetheless have educational value (and are often better produced). Games involve interactive play that teaches goals, rules, structure, adaptation and problem solving, all often represented as a story. There are many types of games, for example, action, adventure, animated tutorial, puzzle, role-playing, simulation, sports, strategy, virtual reality, virtual world and games-based construction learning.

Such games provide feedback and enable learning by giving enjoyment, passionate involvement, structure, motivation, ego gratification, adrenaline, creativity, social interaction and emotion. A "serious game" is a game designed to facilitate learning as well as entertainment (although adults would be well advised not to refer to them as "serious" games in front of the students). Games may be for single players, for two or several players, or be part of a massively arranged system for multiple cooperative teams or adversaries, as in Massive Multiplayer Online Games (MMOGs) (Wikipedia).

Effects of Educational Games

In 2022, Topping et al. found 488 studies of games in school, indicating such investigations were very popular. However, only a portion of these linked games to thinking development. On a vote count, 81% of these studies reported games to be more effective than traditional instruction. Fifty-six reviews of the effectiveness of games were located and 88% of them found games better than traditional instruction, except for two, which found them equivalent, and five studies which were unclear. However, many of these reviews did not distinguish between elementary, secondary and higher education. Only 11 of these reviews gave Effect Sizes, and these ranged from 0.13 to 1.13, with a mean of 0.48.

Topping et al. (2022) give a list (below) of additional conclusions, each based on fewer studies, which may be useful (and a further list of teaching points is given in the supplementary material to the publication):

1. Ease of use, challenge, degree of student control and interactivity are important in effectiveness.
2. The popularity of a game is not necessarily equal to its effectiveness.
3. More student control generally works better in the long run (teachers sometimes have difficulty letting go of control).
4. Collaborative games are more effective than competitive games.
5. Simulation in games is very effective, especially with active engagement.
6. Games can be played individually or collectively, but peers working together outperform individuals.
7. Goal-setting lowers cognitive load and yields more fun – including in peer interactions.
8. Scaffolding and engagement are important, as in every learning task.
9. Provision of specific feedback and encouraging children to think about what strategies they use can improve learning.

10. Concept mapping (i.e., visual representations that students create to connect concepts, ideas, terms) is effective in raising performance.
11. Games with a Teachable Agent (avatar) tend to be more effective than those without.
12. Background music increases effectiveness (even though it appears distracting).
13. Prosocial games improve prosocial behavior.

Turning to reviews that focus more specifically on the relationship between educational games and thinking development, Lamb et al. (2018) conducted a meta-analysis of 46 studies, which found a medium effect for cognition (effect size = 0.67) and affect (effect size = 0.51) with a small effect for behavior (effect size = 0.04). Games and simulations did not differ in effectiveness.

After this, Sun et al. (2021) meta-analyzed 22 studies to determine the effectiveness of using educational games to improve students' critical thinking skills. The results showed that educational games could promote the improvement of students' critical thinking skills (ES = 0.77). The positive connection between educational games and critical thinking skills was affected by sample size, grade level, game usage mode and game tools. Controlling the class size to fewer than 50 students and a more strategic choice of game tools and usage modes were more conducive to promoting students' skills.

Even later, Mao et al. (2022) meta-analyzed 20 studies with 1,947 participants, focusing on the effect of game-based learning on students' critical thinking. Twenty-one effect sizes showed that game-based learning had a significant positive overall effect on students' critical thinking (effect size = 0.86), but with significant heterogeneity among effect sizes. Among game types, role-playing games yielded the largest mean effect size (ES = 1.83). The effect size of game-based learning was larger for critical thinking disposition (1.77) than critical thinking skill (0.66). Game-based learning also had a larger effect on students in collectivistic countries (1.28) than those in individualistic countries (0.43).

Also of interest is the study of Xiong et al. (2022), who used games with pre-school children aged 3–6 years with the aim of developing their creative thinking. A standardized test was used to evaluate this, a rather severe test of generalization. All five test indicators were significantly improved. The effect of student game training on outcomes was evident. This is one example of the many studies of games with very young children.

Theoretical Underpinnings of Educational Games

Studies have confirmed that digital games can improve critical thinking and problem-solving skills and enhance creativity and student performance. Studies also show that game-based learning can improve cognitive level abilities such as attention skills, increased memory capacity, working memory, the ability to store and manipulate spatial images, decision-making speed and assignments. Digital games test thinking skills based on Bloom's cognitive taxonomic levels, that is, remembering, understanding, analyzing, applying, evaluating and creating. Four things need to be taken into account regarding games: things that must be learned (things I must learn), things that can be learned (things I can learn), learning outside the game (external learning) and unexpected learning (coincidental learning).

When playing digital games, players need to do analysis, synthesis and critical thinking to achieve game goals and game planning. Content and how to play require new skills and knowledge that anyone who has never played may never have experienced. Where there are tests and answers to problems that need to be faced and resolved, players need to try with high determination to accomplish the goal. The effort and seriousness shown by the players to achieve the goals of the game indirectly generate creativity and critical thinking, as the players continuously strive with various methods to achieve what is desired. Players will think creatively and give complete focus, attention and concentration while playing, because almost all digital games compel this.

Providing students with choices can increase their enjoyment, as well as self-efficacy, intrinsic motivation, sense of control and task persistence. This, in turn, can lead to better performance in the task at hand. The motivational aspects of choice have been part of many frameworks, including the expectancy-value model of achievement motivation, social cognitive theory, flow theory and self determination theory, which have all been used to explain the psychological aspects of fun associated with games, and highlight user control and autonomy in intrinsic motivation and enjoyment. For example, a study found that children who were given more choices about their representation in a learning game environment exhibited not only more intrinsic motivation, but also greater depth of engagement, as evidenced by a preference for more challenging versions of the game, the greater use of complex operations and an emphasis on strategic play. Presenting ethical dilemmas as choice points in games is becoming a popular game design pattern and using them in classroom environments could provide benefits when preparing students to be informed, engaged and critical individuals.

Feedback is one of the crucial components of video games. For example, many games use visual and auditory feedback to let players know if certain actions have succeeded or failed. Such feedback elements communicate details almost instantly about the game's inner states and its core game mechanics to the player. Players are allowed, repeatedly, to try again if they do not succeed, which is not common in classroom-based learning. In fact, game players are encouraged to evaluate their errors and play again, especially as more arduous challenges occur.

Camerer (2003) notes that game theory is a kind of mathematical language for describing strategic interactions, in which each player's choice affects the payoff of other players (where players can be people, companies, nation-states, etc.). The impact of game theory had been limited by the lack of cognitive mechanisms underlying game-theoretic predictions. "Behavioral game theory" is an approach linking game theory to cognitive science by adding cognitive details about "social utility functions", theories of limits on iterated thinking and statistical theories of how players learn and influence others. New directions include the effects of game descriptions on choice ("framing"), strategic heuristics and mental representation. There are other authors who take an even more mathematical approach to the issue of game theory, but this goes to a level of complexity with which most teachers would not be concerned.

Structure and Implementation of Educational Games

Classroom teachers will not usually consider making games themselves, although there are some interesting studies where teachers have involved students in designing games, with positive outcomes, especially for girls. Kahoot (https://kahoot.com) offers a platform for this, but it costs money. Consequently, this section will focus more on how to choose a suitable game. There is a vast array of games available, so recommendations from other teachers or the literature are needed to investigate games. Teachers need to trial a game by playing it – there is no other way.

Clearly, the age and ability level of the students will need to be considered. Gender may also need to be considered, as some games might be unsuitable for one or the other gender. The extent to which the game uses complex language to deliver instructions or give feedback will also have to be thought about if the intention is to use the game with students for whom the native language is not English. Some games may be culturally inappropriate, either because they portray objects or behavior which are not part of the host culture, or because they portray behavior which is not acceptable in the host culture.

Self-efficacy (confidence) is very important at the start as students are anxious; then its importance declines. Teachers might need to reassure students at the beginning. Games typically have scoring systems that track and display progress. Ensure that this is clear and understandable by students – and also seen as fair. The quality of a game is important – for example, three-dimensional games are more effective than two-dimensional games.

Females tend to like instructive games; males tend to like entertaining, competitive games. With games, "lower ability" students tend to make bigger gains than more average or above average students – because games are not like everyday learning in school. There are games for Autism, Learning Difficulties and Attention Deficit and Hyperactivity Disorder.

Games promote interest and enjoyment but are sometimes difficult to directly relate to the school curriculum. Games can improve attention skills – but the research is less robust on the question of whether this generalizes over time and to other activities. The more you can link the game to the curriculum or other learning objectives, the greater are the chances of generalization. Think about how you will follow up game use, encouraging the students to reflect on what has been learned and how it connects to the curriculum.

Augmented Reality (AR) is an interactive experience of a real-world environment where the objects in the real world are enhanced by computer generated information and can increase enjoyment, curiosity and motivation, help link the game to the real world and improve socialization (especially collaborative versions).

Examples of Educational Games

Quest Atlantis (QA) is an example of a carefully designed game, described as "a game without guns", that both teaches and informs (Barab et al., 2005), using a multiuser environment to establish an "immersive narrative". For students aged 9–12 years, it allows users to travel through virtual spaces to perform educational activities, talk with other users and mentors and build virtual personae. It involves completing "Quests" – engaging tasks that are connected to academic curricular and standards and social commitments. Elementary school students who played QA demonstrated statistically significant learning over time in the areas of science and social studies, and a sense of academic efficacy.

QA experience centers around an intersubjective connection or identification with the narrative of Atlantis about a world in trouble. The story line does not reside in one location or in one form of medium but is spread across various media that come together and are given meaning as the user participates in the fictional game context and investigates relevant personal issues. Participation in QA entails a personal and social engagement with the narrative, as children are asked to contribute experiences, ideas and information to the activists of Atlantis. The mythical backstory and unfolding avenues for participation blur the boundaries between the Atlantian world and local contexts, motivating students to engage in social issues that have local relevance. The progression of quests allows students to go beyond an isolated acquaintance with these issues and with disciplinary content.

Thanks to motion-sensing technologies, such as Nintendo's Wii, games that take advantage of human movement are possible. These capabilities allow players to explore concepts physically as opposed to reading, watching, or hearing descriptions in a textbook, or video or audio presentation. A growing body of research has suggested that changing how players move can impact the concepts they learn in math, geology and physics. For example, a game-based learning environment, River City, implements problem-based science that provides deep inquiry skills and content coverage for middle school children. This immersive environment places players in a 19th century city where they practice being scientists and develop scientific habits of mind (Ketelhut & Schifter, 2011). By interacting with other players and non-player characters, players experience the social practices of being scientists by actually "doing science" in a virtual environment.

The game "Spread of a Rumor" introduces students to the concept of exponential growth. It can be played as the spread of a rumor, or the spread of a virus, and works well in an algebra or modeling course, in a quantitative reasoning course, or in a mathematics class.

Each student gets a card, labeled Round 0, Round 1 and so forth. On one student's card, there is a yes next to round 0, while on the rest of the cards, there is a no. The student with a yes is the student who "knows" the rumor or who has the virus. Students stand up and mill around and must look at one other person's card. If that person's card has a yes, the student who did not have a yes now has one, while everyone else writes no without saying anything about which they have on their card. After enough rounds so that everyone has a yes (for a class of 35, this is usually about 6 rounds), students sit down, and a chart is made of how many had a yes at each round. Connections are then made to doubling and to powers of two, which then leads to a discussion of exponential growth. If the game is played only up to a certain number of rounds, it mimics plain exponential growth (as does the spread of a rumor or virus in a large population). The game can later be played with different growth factors, such as introducing some amount of immunity (a person gets the virus only after being exposed twice, or three times) or increased virulence (each person shows two or three people their card, on each round).

"NIU-Torcs" is an example of a game that allows for deeper mathematical learning (Coller & Scott, 2009), intended to help mechanical engineering students learn numerical methods. Students begin the game by learning how to code acceleration and steering using the programming language C++. Making the car move fast and nimbly without skidding on the road requires students to calculate numerical roots, solve systems of linear equations and be able to do curve fitting and simple optimization. Students are motivated to keep trying far more than when given these types of problems as meaningless homework exercises. Concept maps produced by the students showed that although measures of low-level knowledge were statistically identical between experimental and control classes, students in the game-based class had much greater levels of deep thinking, which included being able to compare and contrast methods and link concepts together.

Training for Educational Games

There is little in the literature about training either teachers or students to use educational games, although an internet search shows a few companies and an occasional university offering online or even face-to-face courses in developing and using games. However, most teachers will be interested in specific games and training on a specific game is less easily available. Each game is so different from the next, when games are used in the class, the teacher must have previous experience of the game in question to be able to coach students who are having difficulty implementing it.

Additionally, some games are better than others at making it clear how to play the game, perhaps through ascending levels of difficulty, and this will be one of the issues for which teachers will be vetting games. Beyond traditional learning paradigms, game-based approaches require cross-disciplinarity, longer class durations, mixed student groups, social learning and team-teaching models to come into place to really capitalize on the merits of games as learning approaches.

Extensions of Educational Games

We have seen that educational games can be for any age or ability level or gender, related to any curriculum subject or to many, and be in any language and adapted to any cultural context. The literature on games is very large, but the take-up within schools is much lower, perhaps because teachers are preoccupied with delivering the traditional curriculum, often in traditional ways. Nonetheless, the research evidence is very positive, so more implementation can certainly be expected. Games might become more complex as time goes on, but insofar as games are expected to be used in schools, the availability of teacher time in vetting them is a major blockage.

References and Bibliography

Barab, S., Thomas, M., Dodge, T., Carteaux, R., & Tuzun, H. (2005). Making learning fun: Quest Atlantis, a game without guns. *Educational Technology Research and Development*, *53*(1), 86–107. https://www.jstor.org/stable/30220419

Camerer, C. F. (2003). Behavioural studies of strategic thinking in games. *Trends in Cognitive Sciences*, *7*(5), 225–231. https://doi.org/10.1016/S1364-6613(03)00094-9

Coller, B. D., & Scott, M. J. (2009). Video game-based education in mechanical engineering: A look at student engagement. *International Journal of Engineering Education*, *25*(2) 308–317.

Ketelhut, D. J., & Schifter, C. C. (2011). Teachers and game-based learning: Improving understanding of how to increase efficacy of adoption. *Computers & Education*, *56*(2), 539–546. https://doi.org/10.1016/j.compedu.2010.10.002

Lamb, R. R., Annetta, L., Firestone, J., & Etopio, E. (2018). A meta-analysis with examination of moderators of student cognition, affect, and learning outcomes while using serious educational games, serious games, and simulations. *Computers in Human Behavior*, *80*, 158–167. https://doi.org/10.1016/j.chb.2017.10.040

Mao, W. J., Cui, Y. H., Chiu, M. M., & Lei, H. (2022). Effects of game-based learning on students' critical thinking: A meta-analysis. *Journal of Educational Computing Research*, *59*(8), 1682–1708. https://doi.org/10.1177/07356331211007098

Sun, L. H., Guo, Z., & Hu, L. L. (2021). Educational games promote the development of students' computational thinking: A meta-analytic review. *Interactive Learning Environments*. https://doi.org/10.1080/10494820.2021.1931891

Topping, K. J., Douglas, W., Robertson, D., & Ferguson, N. (2022). The effectiveness of online and blended learning from schools: A systematic review. *Review of Education 10*(2), e3353. https://doi.org/10.1002/rev3.3353

Turkay, S., Hoffman, D., Kinzer, C. K., Chantes, P., & Vicari, C. (2014). Toward understanding the potential of games for learning: Learning theory, game design characteristics, and situating video games in classrooms. *Computers in the Schools*, *31*(1–2), 2–22. https://doi.org/10.1080/07380569.2014.890879

Xiong, Z. Y., Liu, Q., & Huang, X. Q. (2022). The influence of digital educational games on preschool children's creative thinking. *Computers & Education*, *189*, 104578. https://doi.org/10.1016/j.compedu.2022.104578

Section E
Evaluation, Discussion and Conclusion

Finally, we consider how the effectiveness of thinking skills programs might be evaluated, balancing standardized tests (which may be of doubtful relevance) with customized measures of actual thinking skills (which may be highly situated and raise questions of generalization). We then proceed to a Discussion chapter, which tries to draw together the common threads of the different sections so far. This might give teachers some idea of how to use elements of thinking skills methodology every day in all their lessons, without following any particular program. Appendices follow.

14
Evaluating Thinking Skills Development

Having described the researched effects of programs intended to enhance cognition and how to implement them, teachers might (and should) be concerned with how they know the program that they have implemented has had the desired effect. How will you know if you implemented the program in the same way as the positive research studies?

Sampling and Comparison Groups

First you need to think of what sample you will use – probably just your own class to start with. But if they are going to be the intervention class, you should also have a comparison class who do not participate in the intervention, so you can see whether any improvement could be explained just by students becoming older and more mature. Obviously, the comparison class needs to be as much like yours as possible (other than not having the intervention), so another class of the same grade, similar size, similar ability and somewhat similar gender balance is needed. Don't worry about disadvantaging the comparison class – if you find your intervention works, then you can invite that teacher to join in the intervention. Remember that you will need to apply your measures to the comparison class as well as the intervention class.

Of course, if you are running a larger project with many classes, teachers and schools, it all becomes more complex. You will need to allocate classes to intervention or control group, and do it randomly. Of course, some teachers may not like this, but reassure them that they are not excluded, they just have to wait to participate. On completion, you may find that results vary from class to class. This may be due to different kinds of students in each class, or to variation in implementation by the teacher.

Implementation Integrity

Related to the previous sub-section is the issue of implementation integrity. How will you know that all the teachers involved implemented the program equally well? Do you want to have them complete weekly diaries about how their thinking sessions went? Or do you want to have meetings with them to ask them the same question? (group meetings can sometimes make the slackers improve their performance). Or do you want to have them video thinking lessons periodically and post them so everyone involved can see and discuss what is happening? This latter is more time-consuming but very good for professional development.

Next, we will address how we will know if the intervention is beneficial – what outcome measures might we use? And what about the reliability and validity of these measures?

Questionnaires

Questionnaires are a good way to sample the perceptions of those involved, but try to make the questions specific and about what the respondents did, rather than vague and general. You can use them with large numbers of participants and provided most of the questions are multiple-choice, they are quite easy to score – but remember to also ask some open-ended questions at the end so you can obtain thoughts you have not directly asked about. Also remember that you should ask not just the teachers, but also the students – and maybe even their parents. There is also the issue of whether respondents will just give you the answer they think you want to hear – a particular problem with students in your own class where you are the teacher and the evaluator combined. If you and the comparison class teacher want to swap classes to give the questionnaire, that might help. If the questionnaires are anonymous, this may improve honesty! However, at the end of the day you are only gathering subjective perceptions, which may have rather doubtful connection to what actually happened.

Interviews

Interviews can be very useful to explore what respondents thought in greater depth and give them much more opportunity to say what they want to say rather than follow your set list of questions. However, as before, think about using them with students as well as teachers – and maybe parents. Interviews are much more time consuming to give and subsequently analyze than questionnaires, so you will only be able to find time to do a few of them. If selecting students for interview, make sure you select from all bands of ability and gender – if you only select the high performers, you will introduce bias into the results. You might want to make the questionnaire for students highly structured, so you describe hypothetical learning scenarios and ask students to describe how they would use thinking skills during it. However, at the end of the day you are again gathering only subjective perceptions, which may have a rather doubtful connection to what actually happened.

Diaries

You could ask both the teachers and the students to keep diaries, in which they enter weekly or more often their description of what was done, their reflections on how useful it was and how it could be improved. However, this will take a fair bit of time for them, but even more time for you when you come to analyze them. This gives a good guide to implementation integrity, however (see previous section).

Attitudes and Dispositions

Many errors in thinking occur not because people do not have any thinking skills, but because they do not have the motivation or disposition to use them. Disposition measures seek to estimate willingness to engage in cognitive tasks.

An example is the California Critical Thinking Dispositions Inventory (Facione, 1990). This test measures: truth-seeking, open-mindedness, analyticity, systematicity, critical thinking, confidence, inquisitiveness and maturity of judgement. It was designed for students from 10th grade. It has a 75-item multiple-choice format. Adequate to good internal consistency is reported: 0.60–0.90.

Another is the California Measure of Mental Motivation (Insight Assessment, 2011). This measures four factors: learning orientation, creative problem solving, mental focus and cognitive integrity. It can be used from kindergarten to adulthood. It has good internal consistency (0.73–0.87). Validity studies show some correlation with self-efficacy (0.28–0.40) and academic achievement (GPA 0.19 to 0.46, SAT 0.10 to 0.46).

The Myself–As–A–Learner scale (MALS) was compiled by Burden (1998) to examine children's self-perceptions as learners. The measure comprises 20 self-referring statements such as 'learning is easy' on which students rate themselves on a five-point scale. The statements are read out to all students in a class following a standardized script.

The Taxonomy of Problematic Social Situations (TOPS) was devised by Dodge, et al. (1985) for primary aged pupils. It is a questionnaire that teachers complete to identify the specific social situations or tasks a particular pupil finds difficult. The teacher is asked whether the child experiences difficulties in 44 problematic social situations and rates a child on a five-point scale.

A suite of self-assessment inventories, the Assessment of Learner-Centered Practices (ALCPs), were developed from the American Psychological Association's learner-centered principles (https://www.apa.org/ed/schools/teaching-learning/top-twenty-principles.pdf). Seven scales enabled pupils to evaluate their learning (on a four-point Likert scale) with regard to a range of cognitive and motivational constructs: Active Learning Strategies (cognitive and metacognitive), Knowledge Seeking Curiosity, Task Mastery, Performance-Oriented Goals, Effort Avoidance Strategies, Work Avoidance Goals and Self-Efficacy.

Think-Aloud

Think-Aloud asks students to express their thought processes while doing a particular task, so there is no reliance on retrospection. However, they are still a self-report measure with all the issues that come with that and they may be biased by students' verbal language abilities. Additionally, students may find it hard to articulate their thoughts while doing a task, as this requires multi-tasking, which may be more strongly the case for some students than others.

Observation

There is much to be said for observational measures that look at learners while they are completing a task and estimate their use of thinking skills directly. These have the advantage that they record actual learner behaviors, which allows observers to take non-verbal behaviors into account and record social interactions between learners. They are also less reliant on verbal or language skills, which makes them more suitable for measuring young learners or those with limited language skills. Assessment during task performance appears to be more predictive and accurate than assessment before or after task performance (Dent & Koenka, 2016).

You can observe directly, using an observation schedule you have devised so you know what you are looking for, but this is difficult when you are teaching at the same time. Ideally you need another teacher to take your class while you do the observation. An alternative is to use video recording, but this needs to feature both video of you interacting with the whole class, and video of pairs or groups at work on a task so that you can see that enthusiasm and dialogue that is generated. Do not feel you have to do all the videoing – you can recruit students to do this after briefing them on what you are looking for. However, do not get carried away and record too many videos, because you will find that analyzing them (again using a schedule) takes a long time.

Criterion-Referenced Measures

Criterion-referenced measures check whether the student has achieved a certain criterion of performance on a thinking skills task. Later you ask the student to perform another task (either the same one, in which case there is the danger of a practice effect) or a similar one (in which there is the danger that the so-called similar one is actually not at the same level of difficulty). You can devise your own tasks and method of evaluating performance, which enables you to make the assessment closely aligned with the thinking skills work you have done in class. Or you can use published tests, which will be somewhat un-aligned with your classwork, but will have some of the work done for you.

Burke and Williams (2012) offer two thinking skills assessment approaches. The Assessment of Pupils Thinking Skills (APTS) measure is a 14-item measure of a range of thinking skills and metacognition. The assessment can be used to provide a comparative measure across thinking skills or to provide a sum score of thinking skills and raise metacognitive awareness of thinking skills. It can be used to assess thinking skills interventions and to monitor change in thinking skills over time among 9- to 12-year-olds. The Individual Thinking Skills Assessments (ITSA) are six more in-depth measures of specific thinking skills that can be used before, during or after interventions to provide more detailed information on children's individual thinking skills. The APTS and the ITSA can be used separately or in conjunction to assess change in thinking skills.

Norm-Referenced Measures

Although most tests are designed for Grades 4 and above, some are designed for grades as low as pre-kindergarten (Arter & Salmon, 1987). Most cover a broad grade span. Reliability of these tests is generally good, with coefficients above 0.80. Subtest scores are generally lower. Validity is weak on many of the tests. Not all the tests have norms (making their inclusion in this section something of a mockery), but whether norms collected on a rather small sample will relate to your students is an uncertain question. These instruments vary widely in both purpose and item format.

Examples are as follows:

The Watson-Glaser Critical Thinking Appraisal (NCS Pearson, 2009) measures five factors (inference, recognition of assumptions, deduction, interpretation, argument evaluation). There are short and long forms. Assessment is available online. Reliability is good (Cronbach alpha 0.81–0.89). Convergent validity was quite strong (0.52–0.68). Correlation with GPA was 0.42–0.59 depending on subject.

The 75-item California Critical Thinking Skills Test (Facione, 1990) examines critical thinking dispositions such as: open-mindedness, inquisitiveness, systematicity, analyticity, truth-seeking, critical thinking, self-confidence and maturity. Cronbach's alpha for the overall instrument was 0.92. Administration time is 20 minutes.

The Halpern Critical Thinking Assessment (HCTA, Halpern, 2010) measures five factors (verbal reasoning, argument analysis, hypothesis testing, likelihood and uncertainty and decision-making/problem-solving). It can be administered online and is available in several languages. Test takers are asked to respond to problem-based scenarios and answer open-ended recall-based questions about the scenarios. They then take multiple-choice questions about the scenario (e.g., select the best reason for supporting or not supporting the proposition). It has high reliability

(Cronbach's alpha 0.88) and inter-reliability (0.93). The test also relates to achievement on tests of mathematics (0.50), verbal skills (0.58) and GPA (0.35).

The Cornell Critical Thinking Essay (Ennis 2005) emphasizes argument analysis and respondents are asked to evaluate fictitious letters to newspaper editors. The grading system is somewhat complex. Twenty-four studies of reliability and validity are reviewed by Ennis (2005). Internal consistency is poor (0.59) but inter-rater reliability is high (0.86 to 0.99).

The Cornell Critical Thinking Test (Ennis & Millman, 2005) is a multiple-choice test and measures: induction, credibility, prediction and experimental planning, fallacies, deduction, definition and assumption identification. Split-half reliability ranged from 0.55 to 0.76 and internal consistency 0.52–0.77. The relationship with scholastic aptitude and intelligence measures was quite strong (0.50).

The Cognitive Abilities Test – Third edition (CAT 3) is a multiple-choice test devised by Lohman, Thorndike and Hagen (2001) to assess general reasoning abilities and a pupil's capacity to apply these to verbal, quantitative and non-verbal cognitive tasks. It can be used from ages 8–15 with different forms for each year group. CAT 3 is divided into three batteries – verbal, quantitative and non-verbal – to assess general inductive and deductive reasoning skills in each domain. Each of the three batteries takes approximately 45 minutes to administer. Interior consistency coefficient was 0.76 for the Verbal Battery, .082 for the Quantitative Battery, 0.70 for the Non-Verbal Battery and 0.91 for the overall test. Test-retest correlation was very high.

The Purdue Elementary Problem-Solving Inventory (Feldhusen et al., 1972) tests grades 2–6 students' ability to solve commonsense real-life problems. This test is a general measure of problem solving. There is one form and one level with 49 multiple-choice questions. Students are tested for: Sensing the problem, Identifying a problem, Asking questions, Guessing causes, Clarification of goal, Judging if more information is needed, Analyzing details of the problem and identifying critical elements, Seeing implications, Verification, Solving a single solution problem, Solving a multiple solution problem. The internal consistency reliability of the total score is 0.79.

The Ross Test of Higher Cognitive Processes (Ross & Ross, 1976) assesses the higher-level thinking skills of students in grades 4–6. There is one form and one level containing 105 mostly multiple-choice items. It includes: Analogies, Analysis of Relationships, Deductive Reasoning, Judgments in Terms of Internal Evidence, Missing Premises, Analysis of Elements. Abstract Relations, Derivation of a Set of Abstract Relations, Sequential Synthesis and Production of a Unique Communication. Internal consistency reliability for total score is 0.92; test-retest reliability is 0.94.

Triangulation

More than one method of measurement is of course desirable so that results might be triangulated (compared with each other to see what is common and what is not). Every measure has disadvantages as well as advantages, and by aggregating three (preferably three rather than two) methods, you would hope to cancel out the disadvantages and capitalize on the advantages. Of course, this all takes more time, but it will give you more confidence in your findings. Triangulation also protects you from putting all your eggs in one basket and then being disappointed when you do not get the results you wanted.

Follow-Up

Research studies typically give only short-term answers, as longer-term follow-up is difficult and expensive. But from your perspective as a teacher, you will want to know whether your efforts have resulted in only short-term gains, or whether they have had enduring impact, suggesting you have given your students some skills for life which may sustain them into adulthood. So, you might want to follow up your class after they have gone on to another grade. Of course, you will need the cooperation of the new grade teacher. Using at least one of your triangulated measures (perhaps the one that showed the biggest gains and/or the one that is easiest to administer and analyze), gather some data when your erstwhile students are near the end of their next grade. Of course, be clear about whether the students have received any further thinking skills teaching in the meantime.

References and Bibliography

Arter, J. A., & Salmon, J. R. (1987). *Assessing higher order thinking skills: A consumer's guide*. Portland, OR: Northwest Regional Educational Lab. ERIC number ED 293 877.

Brookhart, S. M. (2010). *How to assess higher-order thinking skills in your classroom*. Arlington, VA: Association for Supervision and Curriculum Development.

Burden, R. L. (1998). Assessing children's perceptions of themselves as learners and problem solvers. *School Psychology International*, *19*(4), 291–305. https://doi.org/10.1177/0143034398194002

Burke, L. A., & Williams, J. M. (2012). Two thinking skills assessment approaches: "Assessment of Pupils' Thinking Skills" and "Individual Thinking Skills Assessments". *Thinking Skills and Creativity*, *7*(1), 62–68. https://doi.org/10.1016/j.tsc.2011.11.002

Dent, A. L., & Koenka, A. C. (2016). The relation between self-regulated learning and academic achievement across childhood and adolescence: A meta-analysis. *Educational Psychology Review*, 28, 425–474. https://doi.org/10.1007/s10648-015-9320-8

Dinsmore, D., Alexander, P., & Loughlin, S. (2008). Focusing the conceptual lens on metacognition, self-regulation, and self-regulated learning. *Educational Psychology Review*, *20*(4), 391–409. https://doi.org/10.1007/s10648-008-9083-6

Dodge, K. A., McClaskey, C. L., & Feldman, E. (1985). Situational approach to the assessment of social competence in children. *Journal of Consulting and Clinical Psychology*, *53*(3), 344–353. https://doi.org/10.1037/0022-006X.53.3.344

Ennis, R. H. (2005). *The Ennis-Weir critical thinking essay test*. Urbana, IL: The Illinois Critical Thinking Project.

Ennis, R. H., & Millman, J. (2005). *Cornell critical thinking test (Level X and Level Z)*. Seaside, CA: The Critical Thinking Company.

Facione, P. (1990). *California critical thinking dispositions inventory*. Millbrae, CA: The California Academic Press.

Feldhusen, J. F., Houtz, J. C., & Ringenbach, S. (1972). The Purdue elementary problem-solving inventory. *Psychological Reports*, *31*(3). https://doi.org/10.2466/pr0.1972.31.3.89

Halpern, D. F. (2010). *Halpern critical thinking assessment*. Mödling, Austria: Schuhfried (Vienna Test System).

Insight Assessment, Inc. (2011). *Critical thinking attribute tests*. Manuals and assessment information. http://www.insightassessment.com/Products/Products-Summary/Critical-Thinking-Attributes-Tests

Lohman, D. F., Thorndike, R. L., & Hagen, E. P. (2001). *Cognitive abilities test* (3rd ed.). Windsor: NFER-Nelson.

NCS Pearson (2009). *Watson-Glaser II critical thinking appraisal: Technical manual and user's guide*. San Antonio. TX: NCS Pearson.

Ross, J. D., & Ross, C. M. (1976). *Ross test of higher cognitive processes: Administration manual*. Novato, CA: Academic Therapy Publications.

Veenman, M. V. J., Van Hout-Wolters, H. A. M., & Afflerbach, P. (2006). Metacognition and learning: Conceptual and methodological considerations. *Metacognition and Learning*, *1*(1), 3–14. https://doi.org/10.1007/s11409-006-6893-0

15

Discussion and Conclusions

This final chapter offers a summary and discussion of the threads that these programs have in common. This may be suitable for busy politicians or school managers to read first. Each main chapter of 12 describing a thinking skills method has been inductively searched for terms relating to the pedagogy of thinking skills. These are listed below, in order of frequency of occurrence in those chapters. The methods using them appear in associated abbreviations.

Peer Interaction (10)
CASE, CGI, PRT, RT, ACTS, TASC, CoRT, P4C, PBL, Games

Discourse, Dialogue, Argumentation (9)
CASE, CGI, PRT, TTG, RT, TASC, CoRT, P4C, PBL

Transfer/Bridging (8)
CASE, RT, ACTS, TASC, IE, CoRT, P4C, PBL

Modeling (7)
This includes modelling/demonstration by the teacher, from peer to peer, or finding models to explain phenomena.
CASE, CGI, PRT, RT, ACTS, TASC, PBL

Scaffolding (7)
PRT, RT, TASC, IE, P4C, PBL, Games

Teacher Role (7)
CASE, CGI, TTG, RT, IE, P4C, PBL

Vocabulary (6)
CASE, ACTS, TASC, IE, CoRT, Games

Reflection (6)
CASE, CGI, ACTS, IE, TASC, PBL

Building on Others' Ideas (6)
CASE, PRT, RT, TASC, IE, P4C

Feedback (6)
PRT, TTG, RT, TASC, CoRT, Games

Questioning (5)
CASE, P4C, PRT, TTG, RT

Prediction (5)
ACTS, RT, TTG, TASC, IE

Judgment, Decision-Making (5)
TTG, ACTS, TASC, IE, CoRT

Self-esteem, Self-efficacy (5)
IE, TASC, CoRT, P4C, Games

Giving/Allowing Time (4)
CGI, PRT, ACTS, P4C

Brainstorming (4)
CASE, ACTS, TASC, CoRT

Explanations (4)
CASE, PRT, P4C, PBL

Strategies, Heuristics (4)
RT, TTG, TASC, Games

Diagrams, Graphic Organizers, Concept Maps (4)
ACTS, TASC, CoRT, Games

Ability of Students (3)
ACTS, CoRT, Games

ZPD/Difficulty (3)
PRT, CASE, TASC

Summarizing (3)
RT, IE, P4C

Mediation (2)
TASC, IE

Training (2)
TASC, IE

Peer interaction and discourse, dialogue and argumentation come to the top of this list. It seems that a great many thinking skills programs depart from a traditional teacher direct instruction model and engage students much more with each other, talking and puzzling out problems.

Three-quarters of the programs are preoccupied with how transfer to other subjects and outside school is going to happen and can be operationalized. Many of the programs involve modeling/demonstration and scaffolding, either from teacher to students or from peer to peer. This implies a substantial change in the role of the teacher.

Half of the programs regard vocabulary (having words to describe thinking acts), reflection, building on another's ideas and giving feedback (whether from teacher to students or from peer to peer) as important. Questioning, prediction and judgment and decision-making are mentioned by nearly half the programs, as is the case with effects on self-esteem, self-efficacy and student confidence (teacher confidence may also rise). The need to give/allow time is mentioned by a third of the programs, and this is clearly likely to be an issue for teachers, especially at the outset. Brainstorming, explanations, strategies/heuristics and concept maps or graphic organizers are also mentioned by a third of the programs.

A quarter of the programs raise the issue of the variation in student ability, even within one class, and the need to adapt problematic challenges to varying zones of proximal development. Where students work in groups, one way of doing this is by having groups of mixed ability, with clear specification of individual roles. Summarizing is also mentioned by a quarter of the programs, while only two programs mention mediation and training, perhaps rather disappointing.

This gives us a picture of the style of teaching thinking skills – a radical departure from the teacher talking most of the time and hardly allowing full student response to any teacher questions, as is often the case in teacher direct instruction as the teacher struggles to cope with the demands of an over-stuffed curriculum that is largely a body of knowledge to be memorized. While teachers are under pressure from school management, district management and government direction to "get through the curriculum" and maximize scores on high stakes tests, change is going to be difficult. However, from time to time, in place to place, creative teachers (and even school management) might slide some thinking skills activity into their operations, in the knowledge that this may well increase achievement as well as thinking skills. Indeed, the list above might inspire teachers to devise their own thinking skills program. Good luck!

Appendix 1

Prompt Sheet 1

Before Reading
"What do the parts of the book tell us?" (Structure)
"What kind of book is it?" (Type)
"How hard is it?" (Difficulty)
"What do you want from the book?" (Reader Aims)

During Reading
"What does the writer want?" (Author Aims)
"What does it mean?" (Meaning)
"Is it true?" (Truth)
"What might happen next?" (Prediction)
"What does it remind us of?" (Links)

After Reading
"What are the main ideas?" (Summarize)
"How do you feel about it?" (Evaluate)
"What did you remember about it?" (Revisit)
"Have you questioned anything else?" (Extend)

Prompt Sheet 2

Before Reading
"What do the parts of the book tell us?" (Structure)
Have you looked at the title and the author? The cover and the pictures?
What do you think the book is going to be about?

"What kind of book is it?" (Type)
What kind of writing is this? Any special kind?
Is it fact (real, information) or fiction (made up, imagination) or something in between?
"How hard is it?" (Difficulty)
Is this book too easy for the tutee?
Is this book too hard for the tutor?
Can we do the "Five Finger test"? (see Tips for Tutors)
"What do you want from the book?" (Reader Aims)
Is this book really interesting to the tutee? Why?
Is it interesting to the tutor?
Are we **sure** we want to go ahead and read it?

During Reading
"What does the writer want?" (Author Aims)
What country, place and time is the book set in?
Who are the main characters and events?
What kind of people do you think the author was writing for?
What do you think the author was trying to do in this book?
"What does it mean?" (Meaning)
What words are especially hard to understand? What sentences?
Can we work it out, or should we look it up, or ask our teacher?
Is there something you need to know which we don't know?
Are you sure you haven't missed it? Should we check?
"Is it true?" (Truth)
Did the book make sense all the way through?
Did anything puzzle or surprise you?
Where is it hard to decide what is fact and what is fiction or opinion?
What do **you** think is true? How do you know that?
"What might happen next?" (Prediction)
What do you think might happen next?
What might make this happen? How likely is this?
Can you imagine or picture in your head what it would look like?

Did the book end as you expected? How else might it have ended?

"What does it remind us of?" (Links)

Does this bit remind you of any bits you have already read? Why?

Does this remind you of anything you already know, or have done yourself?

Does this remind you of any feelings you have had before?

In the future, will having read this be of any use?

After Reading

"What are the main ideas?" (Summarize)

What were the most important points to you?

Can we make a list or map or chart of the main ideas, to help us?

Can we tell another pair the most important points?

Can we think up some questions to make a quiz for other pairs?

"How do you feel about it?" (Evaluate)

Was it any good? What bits did we like best? What bits did we not like at all? Why?

What bits made us think the hardest? What bits seemed most useful or exciting?

Would we tell others in our class to read this?

Would we look for other books of this kind or by this author?

How well did we read and think together on this book? How could we do better?

"What did you remember about it?" (Revisit)

Thinking back to this book, what *did* we remember?

What do we think and feel about it now?

"Have you questioned anything else?" (Extend)

Have we thought about the Paired Thinking Questions when doing any other reading?

Prompt Sheet 3

Before Reading

"What do the parts of the book tell us?" (Structure)

Have you looked to see what is the title and who is the author?
Have you looked at the cover and the pictures?
Have you looked at the date and contents page?
What do you think the book is going to be about?
Have you read anything like this before?
"What kind of book is it?" (Type)
What kind of writing is this?
Is it fact (real, information) or fiction (made up, imagination) or something in between?
Is it a real-life story (biography), science, poem, recipe, news or other special kind of writing?
"How hard is it?" (Difficulty)
Is this book too easy for the tutee?
Is this book too hard for the tutor?
Can we do the "five finger test"? (see Tips for Tutors)
"What do you want from the book?" (Reader Aims)
Is this book really interesting to the tutee? Why?
Is it interesting to the tutor? Why?
What do you want or need from this book?
Are we *sure* we want to go ahead and read it?

During Reading

"What does the writer want?" (Author Aims)

Context

What country and place is the book set in?
Is it about times gone past, what is happening now in the present, or the future?
Who are the main characters?
What do you think the main events are?

Audience

What kind of people do you think the author was writing for?
For example: young or old, clever or ordinary, serious or fun-loving …?

Purpose
What do you think the author was trying to do in this book?
Is there a mission or a quest?
Does the book have a theme or moral?
"What does it mean?" (Meaning)

Word Study
What words does the tutee not understand?
What words do neither of us really understand?
Can we work it out, or should we look it up, or ask our teacher?

Sentence Study
What sentences are especially hard to understand?
Can we work out what it means together, or should we ask someone to help?

Gaps
Was the book hard to read? Why?
Is there something you need to know, which we don't yet know?
Are you sure you haven't missed it? Should we check?
Do the pictures suggest something different or extra to the words?
Is there anything else you would like to know more about?
"Is it true?" (Truth)

Conflicts & Problems
Did the book make sense all the way through?
Did anything puzzle or surprise you?
Are there ideas or events in the book which just don't fit together?
What did the people in the book *feel* about what was happening?
Are there feelings (or values) which just don't fit?

Evidence & Credibility
Can you decide what is fact and what is fiction or opinion?
Where is this hardest?

Where is the evidence for what is said to be fact?
Is there evidence both for and against?
What do you think the author wants you to believe?
Do you believe this?

Solutions
What would your solution to the conflict or problem be?
What would your conclusions or decisions be?
How certain could you be about this?

"What might happen next?" (Prediction)
What do the people in the book want or expect to happen next?
What have you learned about them that helps you to guess what they might do next?
What do **you** think might happen next?
How likely is this?
What might cause this to happen?
Might it depend on something else happening? What?
Can you imagine or picture in your head what it would look like?
Did the book end or conclude as you expected?
How else might it have ended?

"What does it remind us of?" (Links)

Link in Text
Does this bit remind us of any bits you have already read? Why?

Link Back
Does this remind us of anything you already know?
Does this remind you of any feelings you have had before?
Does this remind us of anything you have done or seen in our own life, at school or home or anywhere?
Does this remind you of anything else?

Link Forward
In the future, how might this apply to or be useful in your own life (home, school or anywhere)?

After Reading
"What are the main ideas?" (Summarize)

Find Main Ideas
What were the most important points to you?
What were some key words?
Do we need to read any bits again?

Clarify Main Ideas
Can you say the most important points of the book more clearly?

Sequence Main Ideas
Do we have the most important points in the best order?
Can we make a map or chart of the main ideas to help us?

Re-tell Main Ideas
Can we tell another pair the most important points?
Or should we write it down for the whole class?

Quiz on Main Ideas
Can we think up some questions about the most important points to make a quiz for other pairs?
Can we write it down for the whole class?

"How do you feel about it?" (Evaluate)

Analysis
Was it any good? What bits did we like best? What bits did we not like at all?
What bits made us think the hardest?
What bits did we feel most strongly about?
Did the book turn out to be a good choice for us in the end?
If not, what should we be more careful about next time?

Response
What bits seemed most useful or exciting?
What are we likely to remember best?

Recommendation
Would we tell others in our class to read this?
Would we look for other books of this kind or by this author?

Self-Assessment
How well did we read and think together on this book?
How could we do better on another book?
"What did you remember about it?" (Revisit)
Thinking back to this book, what *did* we remember?
What do we think and feel about it now?
"Have you questioned anything else?" (Extend)
Have we thought about the Paired Thinking Questions when reading any other books?

Prompt Sheet 4

Before Reading

"What do the parts of the book tell us?" (Structure)
Have you looked to see what is the title and who is the author?
Have you looked at the cover and the pictures?
Have you looked at the date and contents page?
Have you looked at the foreword, introduction, chapter titles, headings, index?
What do they tell you about the book?
What do you think the book is going to be about?
Do they make you want to read the book?
Have you read anything like this before?
"What kind of book is it?" (Type) (Genre)
What kind of writing is this?
How do you know?
Is it fact (real, information) or fiction (made up, imagination) or something in between?
Is it a real-life story (biography), science, poem, recipe, news, or other special kind of writing?
Have you read anything like this before?
"How hard is it?" (Difficulty) (Readability)
Is this book too easy for the tutee?
Is this book too hard for the tutor?
Can we do the "five finger test"? (see Tips for Tutors)
Can we read the first page together without difficulty?
"What do you want from the book?" (Reader Aims) (Reader Purpose)
Is this book really interesting to the tutee? Why?

Is it interesting to the tutor? Why?
What do you want or need from this book?
What do you expect from this book?
What do you know already that this book might help with?
Are we **sure** we want to go ahead and read it?

During Reading
"What does the writer want?" (Author Aims)

Context
What country and place is the book set in?
Is it about times gone past, what is happening now in the present, or the future?
Who are the main characters?
What do you think the main events are?
Do you think the author has really known places and people like them?
If not, what sort of time and place did the author come from?

Audience
What kind of people do you think the author was writing for?
For example: young or old, clever or ordinary, serious or fun-loving …?

Purpose
What do you think the author was trying to do in this book?
Is there a mission or a quest?
Does the book have a theme or moral?
What effect do you think the author was trying to achieve?
What do you think the author wants you to believe?
"What does it mean?" (Meaning) (Literal)

Word Study (Vocabulary & Semantics)
What words does the tutee not understand?
What words do neither of us really understand?
Are there any especially interesting or exciting of effective words?

Can we work it out together?
Or should we look it up in the dictionary or ask our teacher?

Sentence Study (Syntax & Semantics, Confusions)
What sentences are especially hard to understand?
Can we work out what it means together?
Or should we ask someone to help? Now or later?
Can we think of a better way of saying it?

Gaps (Comprehension Checking, Elaboration)
Was the book hard to read? Why?
Is there something you need to know, which we don't yet know?
Might the author think you know or believe something when you don't?
Are you sure you haven't missed them?
Should we look back to check?
If they are not there, can we imagine them or make them up?
Do the pictures suggest something different or extra to the words?
Is there anything else you would like to know more about?
Does anything mean or imply more than it says on the surface?
"Is it true?" (Truth) (Critical Judgment)

Conflicts & Problems
Did the book make sense all the way through?
Did anything puzzle or surprise you?
Are there ideas or events in the book which just don't fit together? (Conflict & Contradiction)
What did the people in the book *feel* about what was happening?
Are there feelings (or values) which just don't fit? (Conflict & Contradiction)
Are there sudden changes in the book or surprises? (Constancy and Change)
Does the book have or pose any problems or puzzles?
What is the main one?

Evidence & Credibility
Can you decide what is fact and what is fiction or opinion?
Where is this hardest?
What about the bits which are somewhere in between fact and fiction?
Where is the evidence for what is said to be fact?
How do you know that?
Is there evidence both for and against?
Can you think of any exceptions?
What do you think the author wants you to believe?
Do you believe this?
If so, why? If not, why not?

Solutions
What would your solution to the conflict or problem be?
What would your conclusions or decisions be?
How certain could you be about this? (Probability)
Would this solution or conclusion apply to all people, times and places, or only some?
Which? (Universality vs. Limitation)
"What might happen next?" (Prediction) (Inference & Deduction)
What do the people in the book want or expect to happen next? (Intentionality)
What have you learned about them which helps you to guess what they might do next? (Characterization)
What do *you* think might happen next? (Prediction)
How likely is this? (Probability, Uncertainty)
What might cause this to happen? (Causality)
One cause or more? (Multiple, Complex, Interdependent Causality)
How would you know what had really caused it? (Evidence)
Might it depend on something else happening? What? (Conditionality)
Will it happen *only* if something else happens?
One thing or more than one? (Multiple, Complex, Interdependent Conditionality)

Might there be a biggest or major cause? (Critical Factor or Incident)
If this doesn't happen, what else might? (Alternatives)
Can you imagine or picture in your head what it would look like? (Visual Imagery)
Did the book end or conclude as you expected?
How else might it have ended?
"What does it remind us of?" (Links) (Association, Comparison, Discrimination, Analogy, Classification)

Link in Text
Does this bit remind us of any bits you have already read? Why?

Link Back
Does this remind us of anything you already know?
Does this remind you of any feelings you have had before?
Does this remind us of anything you have done in our own life, at school or home or anywhere?
Does this remind you of anything anyone has told you before (children or adults)?
Does this remind you of anything in another book, on TV or in a film, or anywhere else?
Does this remind you of anything else?
Can you think of any other examples of this kind of thing?
How is what we are reading now similar to these other things?
How is it different?

Link Forward
In the future, how might this apply to or be useful in your own life (home, school, or anywhere)?

After Reading
"What are the main ideas?" (Summarize)
Find Main Ideas (Focus, Prioritize)
Who? Do? What? Where? Why? To? How? With? Then?
What were the most important points to you?

What were some key words?
Do we need to read any bits again?

Clarify Main Ideas (Reformulation, Reconstruction)
Can you say the most important points of the book more clearly?
Sequence Main Ideas (Reformulation, Reconstruction)
Do we have the most important points in the best order?
Can we make a map or chart of the main ideas to help us?

Re-tell Main Ideas (Communicate)
Can we tell another pair the most important points?
Or should we write it down for the whole class?
Should we read our writing to each other before we give it to anybody else?

Quiz on Main Ideas (Interrogate)
Can we think up some questions about the most important points to make a quiz for other pairs?
Can we write it down for the whole class?
Should we read it to each other before we give it to anybody else?

"How do you feel about it?" (Evaluate)

Analysis
Was it any good? What bits did we like best? What bits did we not like at all?
Was it important? What bits made us think the hardest?
What bits did we feel most strongly about?
How could the author improve the book? How would *you* improve it?
How far apart were what *we* wanted and what the author wanted?
Did the book turn out to be a good choice for us in the end?
If not, what should we be more careful about next time?
Response (Application, Generalization, Maintenance)
What bits seemed most useful or exciting?
What are we likely to remember best?

What might we *do* with what we have learned?

Recommendation
Would we tell others in our class to read this?
Would it be good for any other sort of people?
Would we look for other books of this kind or by this author?

Self-Assessment
How well did we read and think together on this book?
How could we do better on another book?
"What did you remember about it?" (Revisit) (Recall, Reflect)
Thinking back to this book, what *did* we remember?
What do we think and feel about it now?
What use has it been, so far?
"Have you questioned anything else?" (Extend) (Application, Generalization, Maintenance)
Have we thought about the Paired Thinking Questions when reading any other books?
In school or out of school? On books read with someone or on your own?

Appendix 2

Studies Showing Positive Effects for PBL in Schools

Aidoo, B., Sampson, K. B., Kissi, P. S., & Ofori, I. (2016). Effect of problem-based learning on students' achievement in chemistry. *Journal of Education and Practice*, *7*(33), 103–108.

Chen, C. M., & You, Z. L. (2019). Community detection with opinion leaders' identification for promoting collaborative problem-based learning performance. *British Journal of Educational Technology*, *50*(4), 1846–1864. https://eric.ed.gov/?id=EJ1223373

Khoiriyah, A. J., & Husamah, H. (2018). Problem-based learning: Creative thinking skills, problem-solving skills, and learning outcome of seventh grade students. *Indonesian Journal of Biology Education*, *4*(2), 151–160. http://ejournal.umm.ac.id/index.php/jpbi

Lee, T. H., Shen, P. D., & Tsai, C. W. (2008). Applying web-enabled problem-based learning and self-regulated learning to add value to computing education in Taiwan's vocational schools. *Journal of Educational Technology & Society*, *11*(3), 13–25. http://www.jstor.org/stable/jeductechsoci.11.3.13

Mulyanto, H., Gunarhadi, G., & Indriayu, M. (2018). The effect of problem based learning model on student mathematics learning outcomes viewed from critical thinking skills. *International Journal of Educational Research Review*, *3*(2), 37–45. https://doi.org/10.24331/ijere.408454

Nay, F. A., & Rudhito, M. A. (2020). Implementation of virtual manipulative using problem-based learning on topic algebra for seventh grade students. *Journal of Physics: Conference Series*, *1470*(1), 012053. https://doi.org/10.1088/1742-6596/1470/1/012053

Ojaleye, O., & Awofala, A. O. A. (2018). Blended learning and problem-based learning instructional strategies as determinants of senior secondary school students' achievement in algebra. *International Journal of Research in Education and Science*, *4*(2), 486–501. ERIC Number: EJ1185068.

Peen, T. Y., & Arshad, M. Y. (2014). Teacher and student questions: A case study in Malaysian secondary school problem-based learning. *Asian Social Science*, *10*(4), 174–182. https://doi.org/10.5539/ass.v10n4p174

Ramadhani, R., Umam, R., Abdurrahman, A., & Syazali, M. (2019). The effect of flipped-problem based learning model integrated with LMS-google classroom for senior high school students. *Journal for the Education of Gifted Young Scientists*, *7*(2), 137–158. https://doi.org/10.17478/jegys.548350

Serungke, M., & Muhibbuddin, S., (2020). Implementation of problem-based learning (PBL) with virtual laboratory to improve students' critical thinking and achievement. *Journal of Physics: Conference Series*, *1460*(1), 012134. https://doi.org/10.1088/1742-6596/1460/1/012134

Sihaloho, R. R., Sahyar, S., & Ginting, E. M. (2017). The effect of problem based learning (PBL) model toward student's creative thinking and problem solving ability in senior high school. *IOSR Journal of Research & Method in Education (IOSR-JRME)*, *7*(4), 11–18. https://doi.org/10.9790/7388-0704011118

Widyatiningtyas, R., Kusumah, Y. S., Sumarmo, U., & Sabandar, J. (2015). The impact of problem-based learning approach to senior high school students' mathematics critical thinking ability. *IndoMS-JME*, *6*(2), 30–38.

For Product Safety Concerns and Information please contact our EU
representative GPSR@taylorandfrancis.com
Taylor & Francis Verlag GmbH, Kaufingerstraße 24, 80331 München, Germany

www.ingramcontent.com/pod-product-compliance
Lightning Source LLC
Chambersburg PA
CBHW070059020526
44112CB00034B/1733